30-DAY IN HIS PRESENCE CHALLENGE THROUGH GENESIS

A THOUGHT PROVOKING AND PRACTICAL DEVOTIONAL COMMENTARY

SEAN ARVISO

COPYRIGHT

Sean Arviso
Visit my website at www.amazon.com/author/seanarviso

Printed in the United States of America

ISBN: 9781091576414

GET CONNECTED!

DO YOU NEED A SPEAKER FOR YOUR EVENT?

Sean would love to serve you by speaking at your church or event on any Biblical or Apologetical topics. Simply email him at sean_arviso@yahoo.com for more information.

GET A FREE BOOK

By joining our Reader's Group you will get a free copy of Sean's book "Fact or Fiction: Is There Evidence to Support the Reliability of the Bible and the Resurrection of Jesus?" To get your copy, email sean_arviso@yahoo.com and say "I would like my free copy of Fact or Fiction!"

GET SOCIAL

Personally connect with Sean through his Facebook, Instagram, and Amazon Pages.

DEDICATION

To Jesus Christ, my Savior and Lord, this work is my sacrifice of worship to You.

To Victoria, my bride, partner, and co-laborer in the Gospel, I pray this work is a blessing to you.

To my kids, both biological and spiritual, I pray this work helps train you to love and serve your Creator.

INTRODUCTION

Have you found it difficult to study the Bible and live like Jesus? Have you been frustrated because you want to follow Christ, but you may not have the practical guidance how to do so? Do you want to get excited to read and study God's word? Whether you're a new Christian, or a long-time follower of Christ, the In His Presence Devotional Commentary Series will give you clear ways to walk with Jesus while equipping you to read and study the Bible effectively in a fresh way that is easy to understand. God has given me the privilege of not only studying in Israel, Peru, and the United States to earn my B.A. in Biblical Studies with a specialization in Apologetics, but to also serve as a pastor where I have seen God change many lives. The truth you will receive in this book will improve all areas of your life; spiritual, mental, physical, and even financial. If you want to experience excitement for God and His word today then I urge you to stop waiting. Don't live another moment missing this opportunity. It's time to get started by taking the 30-Day In His Presence Challenge through the Book of Genesis.

~

HOW TO USE THIS BOOK

My prayer is that you have a strong foundation in the word of God so that you may have a strong relationship with the God of the word. Charles Haddon Spurgeon, the famed 1800's English Baptist preacher, has said, "Visit many good books, but live in the Bible." My desire is that this resource would be one of those "good books" that you visit time and time again as you live your life in and live out Scripture. Here's how to use this book:

Be Consistent - Don't skip a day! As you begin your day, have your Bible open, heart ready to receive from the Lord, and this resource. Read the passage corresponding with what day you are on and then read this resource to go deeper.

Join the Community - As you begin your 30-Day In His Presence Challenge, I want to walk with you through this. So, here's what I encourage you to do: Take a picture of your copy of the book, post on your Social Media (ie. Facebook, Instagram, etc.), tag me using "@seanarviso", and use the #inhispresencechallenge. By doing this I will be at your service to help you along the way, you will be a part of the community, and Lord willing, encourage others to take this challenge with you.

Start or Join a Small Group - Here's a a great way to enjoy this resource with others:

- Discuss what was profound, eye-opening, or important for each person.
- Discuss each person's experience applying the Action Point.
- Read through the Day you're on together.
- Discuss how each person is going to implement that Day's Action Point.

CONTENTS

DAY ONE

INTRODUCTION TO GENESIS

"Why defend Genesis when so many people don't even believe in Jesus? Why not concentrate on defending the big issues, like the Gospel and the deity of Christ? Considering all the problems we have in society, should we really be focused on apologetics, rather than trying to change our culture? It takes time and effort to learn to defend biblical creation. Wouldn't that time be better spent defending the important Christian doctrines, and fighting abortion, gay marriage, racism, and other social ills? Many Christians pose these questions. The debate over origins seems like such a secondary and academic issue compared to the real-life problems we face every day. But what if our failure to defend Genesis is linked to many of these social ills? Is it possible that the problems of our culture stem from the fact that people have rejected the Bible, beginning in Genesis? If so, then defending biblical creation may be the key to resolving these cultural issues." – Dr. Jason Lisle, Astrophysicist

INTRODUCTION TO GENESIS

Before we jump to applying God's word to our lives in this 30-Day In His Presence Challenge, we must first lay a strong foundation that will make this experience richer. I don't want to scare you, but today, the first reading, is going to be a bit heavier on the academic side. Don't worry! Keep reading. I know you can do it. What you're about to receive is more valuable and exciting than you may initially think. So, enjoy!

WHY IS GENESIS SO IMPORTANT?

Well, ideas have consequences. What you believe determines how you think. What you think dictates what you do. What you do dominates your life. Therefore, what you believe dominates your life. What do you believe about the Book of Genesis?

Genesis is the very basis for a biblical worldview. The system of thinking you develop upon your reading and studying of Genesis will directly affect the way you perceive life and live in the world.

The 1st book, and even the 1st statement, of the Bible leaves you as the reader to make a choice; to believe or not to believe.

GENESIS IS THE FOUNDATION OF HISTORY

The book of Genesis gives the only true and reliable account of all basic entities of the universe and of life:

- Origin of the Universe
- Origin of Order and Complexity
- Origin of the Solar System
- Origin of the Atmosphere and Hydrosphere
- Origin of Life
- Origin of Man

- Origin of Marriage
- Origin of Evil
- Origin of Language
- Origin of Government
- Origin of Cultures
- Origin of Nations
- Origin of Religions
- Origin of the Chosen People, Israel

GENESIS IS THE FOUNDATION OF THE BIBLE

How you interpret and understand the book of Genesis will determine how you interpret and understand the rest of the Bible. If your theological foundation is faulty, then your entire theological building built upon it is faulty.

Notice how intertwined the book of Genesis is with the New Testament:

- All books of the New Testament except Philemon, 2nd John and 3rd John contain allusions to Genesis.
- Of the 50 chapters in Genesis, only 6 (20, 24, 34, 36, 40, & 43) are not quoted in the New Testament.
- More than half of the 200 New Testament allusions to Genesis are found in the first eleven chapters of Genesis:
- 63 are to the first 3 chapters of Genesis.
- 14 of the allusions are regarding the Flood.
- 58 references are related to Abraham.
- 25 of these references were from Jesus Himself.

If Jesus quoted the book of Genesis as literal and historical, then so should we!

TIME AND AUTHORSHIP OF GENESIS

There are two different views in regard to the authorship of Genesis:

- The Documentary Hypothesis:

In an attempt to hold onto both evolution and the Bible, many liberal theologians have accepted this view. This is also called the "J.E.D.P. Hypothesis", the letters standing for the supposed writers of the respective portions. The "Jehovist Document", supposedly dated about 850 B.C. was marked by the use of the divine name Jehovah; the "Elohist Document", about 750 B.C. marked by the use of the name Elohim; the "Deuteronomist Document" was supposed to be a further editorial emendation of the first two, dated about 620 B.C., containing especially most of Deuteronomy; and, finally, the "Priestly Document", represents supposed editorial revisions by a group of Jewish priests around 500 B.C.

- Moses wrote the book of Genesis along with the rest of the Pentateuch (First 5 Books of the Old Testament):

There are a few ways that Moses could have received this information:

1. He received it by oral traditions passed down through the generations.
2. He took written records of the past and compiled them under the guidance of the Holy Spirit.
3. He received direct revelation from God.

So which view is true? Well, Jesus believed, according to Luke 24:27, 44 that Moses wrote the book of Genesis and "the Law" which is the Pentateuch; also known as the "Torah" which means "instruction". We can be certain that Jesus knows more than any seminary professor or hardened skeptic.

In regards to the time of the authorship of Genesis, because we know that Moses is the author, the time frame of this writing could have been anywhere between 1446 B.C. – 1406 B.C.

HOW ARE WE TO INTERPRET GENESIS AND THE BIBLE?

What I want to give you now is a crash course on Inductive Bible Study. I hope you're as excited as I am! This is how we must be reading and studying the Bible in order to get the message God has intended for mankind. This is critically important because we must learn to read, study, and apply God's word on our own as well as in fellowship at church, a small group, etc. There are three basic steps: 1) Observation, 2) Interpretation, and 3) Application. Let's get started!

Observation:

When you first read a passage of Scripture, ask the question, "What does the text say?" Not, "What does my pastor say it says?" Or, "What do I think it says?" Simply, "what does the text say"? Read the passage several times and record your first impressions; what did you find interesting, what stood out, what questions do you have, etc. After reading the passage several times, then record the who, what, when, and where. This will take a good amount of diligence to understand what was happening culturally, historically, contextually (Where the passage fits in with the whole of the Bible), etc. By doing a good job on your observation, you will then arrive to the correct interpretation and appropriate application.

Interpretation:

After you have a good understanding of the who, what, when, and where, now we can move into the why. This is where we ask the question, "What does the text mean?".

First, here is what not to do when interpreting the text:

- Do NOT interpret the Scriptures by your experience.
- Do NOT be dogmatic or definitive where the Scriptures are not. Where the Scriptures are silent, you and I must be silent.
- Do NOT rationalize the Scriptures.
- Do NOT over-spiritualize the Scriptures.

In order to answer the question, "What does the text mean?" we must do 3 things. First, we must interpret literally, unless otherwise stated; for example, when the passage uses words such as, "like", or "in appearance", or "as". Secondly, we must always study in context. NEVER read a Bible verse. Always read what the author wrote before and after the passage you are studying. For example, if I wrote you a hand-written letter 10 pages long, but you only read page 5, would you understand my whole message to you correctly? Of course not! We must read God's love-letter to us, the Bible, from cover-to-cover to get His full message. Context is key. Thirdly, Let Scripture interpret Scripture. The Bible is the best commentary on itself. If you have a question on a passage, cross-reference with other relevant passages. Search engines like Google make this very easy today. Here is an important phrase: The Old Testament is the New Testament concealed and the New Testament is the Old Testament now revealed. All of that weird "prophet-talk" of the Old Testament now makes sense in light of the New Testament. This is a big example of letting Scripture interpret Scripture.

Application:

Now that you've built a good foundation of understanding the text in observation and interpretation, let's move onto the final step of Application. This is the easiest to understand and the hardest to do. This is where we ask the big question, "How should I respond to this passage?" We answer questions such as, "What examples do I follow or not follow? What is counted as sin and must be forsaken? What errors must be avoided? What promises of God's word have I found? What commands do I obey and what actions must be taken?" This is where we move from being hearers of the word to being doers of the word according to James 1:22.

AUTHORITY: WHO IS IN CHARGE AND WHO IS ACCOUNTABLE?

The issue in regard to Genesis and the Bible, for both believers and unbelievers, is, "Who is the authority? Is God the authority, or am I? Is the Bible trustworthy, or is it not?" Though the purpose of this book is not to defend the reliability of the Bible, if you would like straightforward answers and evidence on that topic, I encourage you to get my other book, Fact or Fiction for free. Please go to the "GET CONNECTED" section at the beginning of this book for more information.

If man is in charge, then you are only accountable to yourself, but if God and the Scripture are in charge, then you are accountable to God.

GENESIS SETS THE STAGE FOR ETERNITY

This is a particularly fun aspect of the Bible! Notice how there are correlations between the First Order (Garden of Eden) and the Final Order (Heaven).

First Order

- Division of Light & Darkness (Genesis 1:4)
- Division of Land & Sea (Genesis 1:10)
- Rule of Sun & Moon (Genesis 1:16)
- Man In A Prepared Garden (Genesis 2:8,9)
- River Flowing Out of Eden (Genesis 2:10)
- Gold In The Land (Genesis 2:12)
- Tree of Life In The Garden (Genesis 2:9)

- Bdellium & The Onyx Stone (Genesis 2:12)
- God Walking In The Garden (Genesis 3:8)

Final Order

- No More Night (Revelation 21:25)
- No More Sea (Revelation 21:1)
- No Need of Sun & Moon (Revelation 21:23)
- Man In A Prepared City (Revelation 21:2)
- River Flowing From God's Throne (Revelation 22:1)
- Gold In The City (Revelation 21:21)
- Tree of Life Throughout The City (Revelation 22:2)
- All Manner Of Precious Stones (Revelation 21:19)
- God Dwelling With His People (Revelation 21:3)

ONE DAY, you and I will go to meet God. He will embrace us and we will embrace Him. The Creator and created no longer separated. Until that day, let us strive to know Him and make Him known by being diligent students of His word and relentless doers of His word.

REDEMPTION GROUNDED WITHIN THE BOOK OF GENESIS

Before Genesis, redemption was **planned**. Within Genesis, redemption was **promised**. After Genesis, redemption was **accomplished**.

Before the writing of the book of Genesis, before the events it records, and even before the Universe began, God already had our redemption through Jesus Christ planned out. We will discuss this more on Day 7 when we look at the 7 Covenants of the Bible, but for today, simply reference the following passages with regard to this: John 1:1 – 3; Ephesians 1:4; 2nd Timothy 1:9; 1st Peter 1:20; Revelation 13:8.

Within the book of Genesis we find the beginning of God being a missionary to us; people who were lost, broken, and without hope. In Genesis 3:15 we find the first promise of a Savior who would be born of a woman, defeat Satan, and bring salvation to mankind. In Genesis 12:1 – 3 we see where the Savior would come from; He would be a Jew from the people of Abraham. In Genesis 49:10 we see that the Savior would come from the tribe of Judah. This, and many more passages within the book of Genesis we find many *shadows* or *types* of Jesus.

After the book of Genesis, we are struck with the reality that God fulfilled His promises and our redemption was accomplished on the cross of Christ and through His resurrection (Luke 2:11; Galatians 4:4 – 5; Hebrews 1:1 – 3). Before we even read the first verse, we must understand that God is setting the stage for the greatest moment in the history of the Universe; the life, death, and resurrection of Jesus Christ.

It is all grounded in Genesis.

IS THE BOOK OF GENESIS RELEVANT TO US TODAY?

Absolutely. Genesis is a book of beginnings; yet, it has much to say about the world in which we live today. Why is the world in the state that it is in? We have answers here in Genesis. Is there any hope for a lost and dying world? Absolutely, the Gospel of Jesus Christ.

If you made it this far, I'm proud of you! We have now laid a good foundation for not just our 30-Day In His Presence Challenge through the Book of Genesis, but also for our time in the Bible as a whole. I guarantee that if you faithfully complete this 30-Day Challenge, you will have certainly strengthened your Christian life.

Let's pray, *"Dear God. You are truly awesome. There are no amount of words that could be spoken, songs that could be sung, films that could be made, or books that could fully explain and display who You truly are. Help me to be a diligent student of Your word and a relentless doer of Your word. During this 30-Day Challenge, please speak to me and transform me to look more like Jesus and less like myself. Thank You that my salvation was planned before, promised in, and accomplished after the book of Genesis. Prepare me for what is ahead; both today and every day You give me. I ask this in the name of Jesus. Amen."*

ACTION POINT

At the end of each day's reading there will be an "ACTION POINT" which will help you apply the truth you are receiving from God's word and gain the most from this resource. Here is your action point for today:

1) Commit to completing this 30-Day In His Presence Challenge through the book of Genesis. Don't skip a day, be consistent. Find a time in your day (Preferably when you first wake up) to consistently have a date (Or meeting) with Jesus and keep it!

2) Get accountable! Think of someone right now who you think would benefit by taking this challenge with you. Contact them right now (Yes, seriously, right now!) and say, "I would love to complete this 30-Day In His Presence Challenge with you!" Of course, use your own words and personality. Without accountability, working with a partner, or in a small group setting, it will be very easy to simply read God's word, this resource, but not actually follow through with applying it. I know you may be a little nervous at today's action point, but I guarantee you, it will be worth it. Go on. Take a step of faith. You won't regret it.

DAY TWO

GENESIS 1:1 - 25

"Why apologetics? Well, the Bible commands it, the culture demands it, the Church needs it, and the results confirm it. Taken individually, each reason should motivate us to engage in apologetics. However, taken all together, these provide a powerful apologetic for apologetics." - Tim Barnett, Apologist with Stand To Reason

IT HAS OFTEN BEEN SAID that if you can believe the first verse of the Bible, then you should have no problem believing the rest of the Bible. This is foundational. The Bible is not a science book (Though science and the Bible are compatible), nor does it explain God's existence, but merely declares it. If God exists, then miracles are possible. If God exists, then the resurrection of Jesus is possible. If God exists, then the claim of the Bible being the word of God is possible. However, does God *really* exist?

ARGUMENTS FOR THE EXISTENCE OF GOD

In Western culture, we are not often physically persecuted like many of our brothers and sisters in Anti Judeo-Christian countries; however, we are absolutely under intellectual persecution. There are many who attack the existence of God, reliability of the Bible, and the establishment of God's Church, etc. My goal for the In His Presence Devotional Commentary Series is not to be completely academic and filled with Christian Apologetics; however, because we are currently going through Genesis together, it's important to bring up the following.

I would like to give you three arguments for the existence of God. There are many more, but let's cover the basics. These will not be exhaustive explanations, but should be effective tools in your Christian tool-kit.:

Cosmological Argument: "Cosmological" comes from the Greek word *kosmos* which means world. The argument goes like this, "Whatever begins to exist had a cause. The Universe began to exist. Therefore, the Universe has a cause." Nothing can cause itself into existence, including the Universe. The 2nd Law of Thermodynamics (AKA – Entropy) states that all usable energy is becoming less usable through heat exchange. In other words, the entire Universe is in a state of decay and winding down. However, if it is winding down, then that means it was "wound up" sometime in the past, and therefore, having a beginning. What, or Who, wound up, or began, the Universe? Something or *Someone* outside of the Universe must've caused it into existence.

Teleological Argument: "Teleological" comes from the Greek word *telos* which means purpose or design. The argument goes like this. "Design implies a designer. The Universe manifests design. Therefore, the Universe has a designer." A watch implies a watchmaker. A painting implies a painter. A building implies a builder. The Universe implies a "Universe-maker". Even Richard Dawkins, a very outspoken atheist of our time, says, "Some species of the unjustly called primitive amoebas have as much information in their DNA as 1,000 Encyclopedias." Our Earth is so finely tuned to support complex life that it is a statistical impossibility we exist. You are literally a miracle! Finally, think about this. Life *cannot* come from non-life. Order *cannot* come from non-order. Intelligence *cannot* come from non-intelligence. Something *cannot* come from nothing.

Moral Law Argument: The argument goes like this, "Moral laws exist. Laws are given. Therefore, there must be a Moral Law Giver." The moral argument begins with the fact that all people from all cultures and from all time periods recognize some moral code (that some things are right, and some things are wrong). Every time we argue over right and wrong, we appeal to a higher law. Right and wrong imply a higher standard or law, and law requires a lawgiver. Because the Moral Law transcends humanity, this universal law requires a universal lawgiver. This, it is argued, is God. Listen to the words of C.S. Lewis from his book Mere Christianity, "My argument against God was that the universe seemed so cruel and unjust. But how had I got this idea of just and unjust? A man does not call a line crooked unless he has some idea of a straight line. What was I comparing this Universe with when I called it unjust?" Here's a Fun Fact: The problem of evil is actually an argument FOR the existence of God. Check out the resources in today's Action Point to find out more.

IN THE BEGINNING

"In the beginning" – The Hebrew word used for this is *bereshith* is the beginning of reality as we know it. The perfect tri-universe that was once in the thoughts of God now spoken into actuality. Perfect bliss. Everything in harmony. No sin. No moral darkness. Only the purity of creation still warm of the breath of its Creator. It's important to note that God is into the number 3; He is a triune being (Father, Son and Spirit, we are a triune being (Body, soul, and spirit), and God created the tri-universe composed of time, space, and matter. You cannot have time without space and matter, you cannot have space without time and matter, and you cannot have matter without space and time. Each are interdependent upon one another.

"God" – The Hebrew word used here is *Elohim*. *El* means God while the Hebrew suffix *im* implies plurality; thus, we are seeing the first evidence of the Trinity.

"created" – The Hebrew word used here is *bara* and it describes *ex nihilo* which is Latin for "creating out of nothing". Only God can do this; make something a reality without need of prior material. There are three important Hebrew words I want us to keep in mind; *bara* (Creating out of nothing), *asah* (Making with material), and *yatsar* (To form). We'll discuss this more tomorrow.

"the heavens" – The Hebrew word used here is *shamayim* which, by definition, simply means "space". There are three "heavens" that the Bible refers to: 1) First Heaven: Earth's Atmosphere (Deuteronomy 11:17; 28:12; Judges 5:4; Acts 14:17), 2) Second Heaven: Outer Space (Psalm 19:4 – 6; Jeremiah 8:2; Isaiah 13:10), and 3) Third Heaven: Paradise or commonly referred to as simply, "Heaven" (1st Kings 8:30; Psalm 2:4; Matthew 5:16).

"the earth" – The Hebrew word used here is *eretz* which means ground or land. It's important to remember that there was no form yet; thus, this refers to the basic elements of matter used to create the Earth.

"without form and void" – The Hebrew phrase used here is *tohu waw bohu* and reveals something spectacular. At this point God has spoken the elements of the Universe into existence, but there is no organization... yet. What does this mean for you right now? Just as God was able to take the unorganized mess of elements to form something beautiful and good, so God wants to take the mess of your life and form something beautiful and good.

Hang in there, my friend. He's working behind the scenes of your life.

"Spirit" – The Hebrew word used here is *ruach* which is used for the 3rd Person of the Trinity, but also translates to wind or breath.

"hovering" – The Hebrew word used here is *rachaph* which means moving, fluttering, or energizing. God, by His Spirit, is now beginning to energize His creation. Science and the Bible are harmonious because God is the Author of the Universe that science observes. The 1st Law of Thermodynamics states that energy cannot be created nor destroyed which correlates with what the Bible states, that God created, and placed, that energy into His Universe.

"Then God said" – This is the first record of God speaking in the Bible. All throughout Scripture, when God has spoken something to be true, it is. If He said it, that settles it. Here's the 21st century comforting truth. If God has been faithful in the past, He will not stop being faithful in the future. Make that universal truth personal for you: If God has been faithful in your past, He will be faithful in your future. It's time to let go of worry. You don't know what the future holds, but you know Who holds the future.

"'Let there be light': and there was light" – Imagine the amount of power God unleashed and it was as easy as speaking a word! Light particles came booming from the mouth of God at about 186,282 miles per second (Speed of light). To give you an idea of how fast that is, light can travel around the Earth 7.5 times in one second. Throughout the Bible we will see light associated with Christ, the word of God, God's people, and God's blessing, while darkness is associated with Satan, sin, death, spiritual ignorance, and divine judgment. Just as God powerfully brought light into the darkness of His creation, so He wants to powerfully shed light on the dark areas of your life. Let no door in your heart be closed to Him.

"evening and morning" – A system of time has now been implemented. Remember, the Earth, though unformed completely, was currently in a state of some sort of watery sphere.

IT's important to remember what we initially stated today, that Jesus is the source, sustainer, and purpose of all creation. Every element, atom, molecule, and organism within the Universe is commanded to worship and lift up its Maker. As we close today's reading, let's finish with this thought: God owns you. Yes, the Bible says God is in relationship to the Christian as a Bridegroom, Father, Friend, Comforter, and more, but He is also your Master (Romans 6:22). In the same way that He commands His creation and it obeys, may we also hear the voice of God from His written word and His still small voice (1st Kings 19:11 – 13) to obey without question and without hesitation.

LET's PRAY, *"Dear God, You are so much greater than I can imagine. Your power is beyond comprehension, Your intelligence is beyond anyone's ability to grasp, and Your love for me doesn't make sense. Who am I in the vast expanse of the Universe You spoke into existence? I don't know why You love me, a sinner, like You do, but I am beyond words thankful. Thank You for pursuing Me, saving me, and desiring to use me for Your glory. Help me to obey You without question and without hesitation just like Your creation does. When I learn from Your word what I should and shouldn't do, help me to take action in intentional and practical ways. Help me to love You like You love me. I ask this in the name of Jesus. Amen."*

∽

ACTION POINT

At the beginning of today's reading we spoke about how the Christian worldview is under intellectual attack in Western civilization; therefore, we need to learn to defend against these assaults with truth, love, and respect. Whether you're a savvy Christian Apologist, or you have no idea what Apologetics even is, here is today's task: Get familiar with Christian Apologetic resources. There are many, but here are seven I recommend. Take some time to go online and check out their resources:

- Cross Examined
- Stand To Reason
- Ravi Zacharias International Ministries
- Christian Apologetics & Research Ministry
- Christian Research Institute
- Evangelical Philosophical Society
- Apologetics.com

By following today's Action Point you will be fulfilling 1st Peter 3:15, "But sanctify the Lord God in your hearts, and <u>always be ready to give a defense</u> to everyone who asks you a reason for the hope that is in you, with meekness and fear." This is an important way to love God with our mind. (Matthew 22:37)

DAY THREE

GENESIS 1:26 - 2:7

"The yearning to know what cannot be known, to comprehend the incomprehensible, to touch and taste the unapproachable, arises from the image of God in the nature of man. Deep calleth unto deep, and though polluted and landlocked by the mighty disaster theologians call the Fall, the soul senses its origin and longs to return to its source." – Aiden Wilson Tozer, Pastor & Author (1897 - 1963)

SABBATH

"He rested on the seventh day" – It's important at this point to discuss the topic of the Sabbath. The word Sabbath comes from the Hebrew word *Shabbot* which means to cease working or to rest. There are three different Sabbaths throughout the Bible:

- The personal Sabbath of the LORD – God does not *need* to rest (Isaiah 40:28), yet the answer for *why* He rested is found in Genesis 1:31, "... He saw everything that He had made..." He had finished his work. Notice two things about God's Sabbath: 1) This is the only day the Bible records He blessed and 2) This is the only day the Bible records He sanctified (set apart). God *resting* here was to model for us how we must live: Work hard throughout the week and then choose a day, or set apart time, to recharge and relax. Now this does not mean to necessarily read your Bible for 8 hours straight or sleep all-day. However, schedule time in your week to slow down and rest in the Lord. Yes, self-care must be a priority in the Christian life (Just don't get carried away and spoil yourself all the time!).

- The national Sabbath of Israel – The first mention of the word Sabbath is in Exodus 16:23. God relates the Sabbath between their bondage in Egypt, God delivering them, and their "rest" in the Promised Land (Deuteronomy 3:20; 12:10; 25:19; Joshua 24:4). Also, every 7 years the nation of Israel was to give the land its Sabbath (Leviticus 25). Israel actually went under God's judgment by being exiled to Babylon for 70 years because of their disobedience to keep the Land Sabbath for 490 years while they lived in Canaan (2nd Chronicles 36:14 – 21; Jeremiah 17:19 – 27; 25:11 – 12; 29:10 – 14). At this point many were living in idolatry and disobeying in other ways as well.

- The ultimate Sabbath of the Christian – When Israel entered the Promised Land and God told them they have entered rest (Deuteronomy 12:9 – 10), this was to really foreshadow and prophecy something of greater importance. Egypt represents sin, Israel represents us as the people of God, the wilderness represents the world we live in, the Promised Land represents Heaven, and Joshua represents Jesus. These are all real places, people, and events, but God orchestrated them in such a way to foreshadow something greater to come. The fact that one day God would take us out of our own Egypt, our own lifestyles of sin, to make us His people who would be faithful laborers in the wilderness called this world until one day Jesus would take us into eternal rest, our Promised Land, called Heaven. At your convenience, take a moment to read Hebrews 3 – 4 discussing how Jesus is the one who brings us into the ultimate rest of Heaven. But wait, it gets better! Jesus offers you rest right now. At times you're troubled, tired, broken, heavy-hearted, and it is at that very moment He sweetly calls you into His arms to find peace in the midst of the storm.

THE NAME OF GOD

"LORD" – The Hebrew here is known as the Tetragrammaton, or translated "YHWH" in English. This word occurs about 6,500x in the Old Testament and the Jewish writers meant for this to be the exclusive name for the God of Israel. There is a small problem for us in modern times; no one on Earth knows how this is truly pronounced. Due to Exodus 20:7, Leviticus 24:16, and many other passages describing the holiness of God's name and how death would be earned to the one who blasphemed this holy name; no one said His name anymore. In ancient Hebrew language, there are no vowels, so all we English speakers have to work with is "YHWH", which is where we get the word "Yahweh". However, it is highly unlikely this pronunciation is the true exclusive name of God given thousands of years ago. The New Testament, which was written in Koine Greek, does not have an equivalent for the Hebrew Tetragrammaton; thus, the New Testament word uses the word *kyrios* for our English word "Lord". So, everywhere in the Old Testament when you see "LORD" in all capital English letters, that is the exclusive name for the God of Israel, and rightly, all of creation.

THE CREATION OF MANKIND

"the LORD God formed man" – The Hebrew word for "formed" is *yatsar* which means to form, to fashion, or to mold. It has the connotation of a potter forming the clay with their hands (Isaiah 64:8) or a knitter with their material stringing together thread by thread to make their masterpiece (Psalm 139:13). This is personal. This is detailed. God invested precision detail into the human body.

"of the dust of the ground" – Here we see the greatness of man, which is being made in the image of God, and we see the lowliness of man, which is being made from dirt. Notice what is not given in Genesis 2:7; the description of man's body. Why is that? It's because God has created every individual uniquely. There is no standard of beauty because everyone is beautiful in the eyes of their Creator. Where there is comparison, there is no contentment. So do yourself a favor and stop comparing yourself to other peoples' looks, popularity, financial status, etc. Don't try and be someone else. Be content with how God made you. Be joyful that you are unique. Be excited that you have a specific plan from God that no one else has. God has precisely designed a blueprint for your life. Now walk in it.

"breathed in his nostrils the breath of life; and man became a living being" – Just as the spirit of God was breathed into Adam to give him physical life, so it is not until the Spirit of God is within someone that they are truly alive. The Gospel of Jesus is not about making bad men become good. It is about making dead men become alive.

From here, after God fashions man and woman, we will see Him working in the life of mankind all the way to the book of Revelation.

. . .

Let's pray, *"Dear God, how incredible You are! Words cannot fully express the praise You deserve. Thank You for creating me uniquely and with astonishing design. Please help me to see the value You have not only placed upon me, but upon everyone. As Your creation, You are worthy of my love, worship, and obedience, so please help me to give that to You freely. You have called me to honor You in work, but You have also called me to honor You in rest. Please show me how You want me to balance work and rest today and for the rest of my life. Please give me Your wisdom, for Your name's sake. I ask this in the name of Jesus. Amen."*

∾

ACTION POINT

Earlier we spoke about the Sabbath, but how do we practice Biblical rest today? Your Action Point today is to Schedule and Strategize Biblical rest into your life:

Schedule – Begin considering how you can schedule daily, weekly, and annual rest into your life. For daily, schedule 1 – 2 hours of personal rest or personal investment. For weekly, schedule a day where you minimize stress and increase rest. For annual, schedule 1 – 2 weeks where you can take a vacation, recharge, and refocus. This can be time of reflection and review of the past 12 months to better pray and prepare for the next 12 months. I understand everyone's work, financial, family, and life situations are different, but ask God to show you how this can be done properly and tailored to your specific season of life.

. . .

STRATEGIZE – I want to focus on strategizing weekly rest into your life. Here are a few ideas to start implementing:

1) Uninterrupted time with God. It's important to daily be in His presence through prayer and His word, but during your rest day, carve out some extra time to go on a date with Jesus (and keep it!). Don't bring your phone to this date, don't be with other people, and limit your distractions. Learn to love to be alone with Him.

2) Unplug from technology. Take it easy on social media (I know you can do it!), walk away from Netflix, put down the video game controller, and practice an activity that doesn't involve technology or a screen. Go for a walk, read a book, connect with God's people over coffee (or a meal!), etc.

3) Make a list of things you would like to do if you had no responsibilities. What would you do if you had no deadlines to meet, no dishes to wash, or no obligations to fulfill? Write them down and then do something on that list!

DAY FOUR

GENESIS 2:8 - 25

"The woman was not made out of his head to rule over him, nor out of his feet to be trampled by him, but out of his side to be equal with him, under his arm to be protected, and near his heart to be beloved." – Matthew Henry, Pastor & Author (1662 - 1714)

THE FIRST MARRIAGE

"...I will make him a helper comparable to him." – Notice how God is the one taking initiative in the fashioning of this marriage. This is an important lesson for all those who have the desire to marry; make sure God is the one starting the process and not your emotions, peer pressure, lust, etc.

"the LORD God... brought them to Adam to see what he would call them." – Because Adam was the first, and perfect, human being, he would have been unspotted from sin and the diseases thereof; thus, allowing him to perform this task quickly and efficiently. Remember, he is only naming each "kind" of animal and not the myriad of different species.

"But for Adam there was not found a helper comparable to him." – As Adam performed his God-given task, undoubtedly he became sharply aware that not only was he unique and superior to the animals, but he was also alone. Little did Adam know God already had a plan. Little do we know God is constantly working in the background of our lives, and even when our hope seems to slip away, God provides at just the right moment and in just the right way. Hold on my friend. Keep doing what God called you to do. He has a plan. You'll see.

"...the LORD God caused a deep sleep to fall on Adam..." – God is now performing the first surgery. There are important nuances in the subtlety of the text. Notice how Adam is not awake during this process; he doesn't know what he needs or what he wants. God is working independently of Adam's desire and will gift him with just the right woman. In the same way, don't rush ahead of God and don't dig your heels in not moving where He wants or you just might miss God's best for you; not only with regard to marriage, but in all aspects of life.

"... He took one of his ribs..." – The Hebrew word for "rib" is *tsela* and it means from the side. This does not literally mean a rib was removed (Though that could still be true); rather, God took part of Adam's bone, flesh, and blood. According to Genesis 2:23 and Leviticus 17:11, life (*nephesh*) is in the blood. Notably, all of mankind came from one woman, but the first woman came from man (1st Timothy 2:13). Men and women were created to walk together, work together, serve together, and love their Creator together.

"...and He brought her to the man." – This is the first wedding ceremony. As we will see, marriage was the only thing we were able to take out of the Garden of Eden. I want to bring light to an attribute of God that is often overlooked. As Christians, we would agree that God is All-Powerful (Omnipotent), All-Present

(Omnipresent), All-Knowing (Omniscient), etc. but He is also All-Romantic. God authored romance, love, and marriage; therefore, it is best done His way. God's commands are not to prevent your joy, but to protect and promote it.

"And Adam said…" – Genesis 2:23, correlated with 1st Corinthians 11:8 – 9 and Ephesians 5:22 – 33, we see God setting the stage for spiritual authority in the home. Both man and woman are created equally important and valuable; however, men have the God-given responsibility of being the leader in the home. In recent times this has been challenged heavily in Western culture with the Feminist Movement of the 1960's to today. Satan knows that if the family unit is deteriorated, you will see the breakdown of the rest of society. It is the Church's job to uphold Biblical marriage if we are to protect and promote the well-being of our culture.

"… man shall leave father and mother…" – Obviously, Adam and Eve didn't have parents; thus, God was looking forward and showcasing Adam and Eve as the model for all future marriages. The marriage relationship is intended to be the strongest relationship on Earth, second to our relationship with the Lord. Marriage is leaving your old family unit to be joined in oneness with your spouse to start an entirely new family unit.

"… be joined to his wife…" – There are many men and women who do not fully join to their spouse. They still want to be babied by their parents, or their friends take priority, or their hobbies and self-interests get in the way of marriage. What a shame that vacation in the mind of some married people is to get away from their spouse for awhile. May this never be so for God's people! Just the opposite, we should look forward to spending time with our spouse, laughing with them, hearing about their day, and intentionally seeking to not only better understand, but to better serve them out of love.

"…they shall become one flesh." – Polygamy, concubinage, polyandry, easy divorce, adultery, promiscuity, and other distortions of the marriage covenant have permeated the world. However, Jesus said in Matthew 19:8, "...but from the beginning it was not so." Marriage is to be a permanent bond, and if you separate, you will tear. Those who have suffered divorce, children of divorced parents, or those in close relationship with a divorcee, knows the severe pain such an event can bring.

"...they were both naked... and were not ashamed." – Everything was perfect. No concept of sin, crookedness, evil, or perversity.

It is appropriate at this time to give an overview of the importance and purpose of marriage from a Biblical point-of-view. Here are 10 points to consider:

1. To populate the world (Genesis 1:28; 9:1)
2. To provide companionship (Genesis 2:24; Matthew 19:4 – 6)
3. To provide proper sexual union (Exodus 20:14; 1st Corinthians 7:2 – 3; Hebrew 13:4)
4. To provide protection for the woman (Malachi 2:15; Ephesians 5:28 – 29)
5. To provide children (Psalm 127:3; 128:3)
6. To avoid sexual immorality (Proverbs 5:15 – 19; 1st Corinthians 7:2 – 4, 9)
7. To be blessed from the Lord (Proverbs 12:4; 18:22; 31:10)
8. To actualize the roles of husband and wife in God's covenant (Malachi 2:14)
9. To establish order in the family (1st Corinthians 11:3; Ephesians 5:23)
10. To represent the Church's union with Christ (Ephesians 5:23 – 25)

As we finish today's reading together, we have been given a

glimpse into what life was like in the Garden of Eden and a look at the first marriage.

LET's PRAY, *"Dear God, I can only imagine what it must've been like to walk in Your creation untouched by the filth of sin. I look forward to the day I get to leave the darkness of this world to enter into the light of Your presence. I know that the world has many opinions regarding romance, relationships, and marriage, but please help me to get my advice from Your unchanging word instead of the constant changing ideas of mankind. Thank You for the beauty of marriage and what it represents. I pray You would strengthen all marriages around the world, and that, more importantly, their goal would be to be pleasing to You. I ask this in the name of Jesus. Amen."*

ACTION POINT

Here is your Action Point for today. If ...

... YOU'RE MARRIED – Find a spiritually mature Christian couple who has been married for many years and seek a friendship with them. If you're a male, connect with the husband, and if you're a female, connect with the wife. Get out of your comfort zone and treat them to coffee or a meal and let them know you want to talk about marriage. Ask questions with the purpose of gaining practical advice on how to better improve your own marriage. Ask questions like, "What advice would you give yourself if you were my age? What resources do you find helpful for a Christian husband/wife/couple? How can I better love and respect my spouse? Etc." You will not only gain rich, battle-tested, tactics and wisdom, but you will also build a friendship with those older than you who have significant life experiences to speak from.

... YOU'RE SINGLE – Start praying for your future spouse. If you really care, choose a day to weekly fast for your future spouse. Pray that God saves them, matures them, prepares them, and that you both wait patiently until He brings you together in His perfect timing.

FOR BOTH MARRIED and Single Christians I recommend exploring the resources of Focus on the Family to receive plenty of useful content. We cannot allow Satan and his influence on the world to win the war on the family. It's time to suit up and fight for your marriage or future marriage.

DAY FIVE

GENESIS 3:1 - 24

" **S** in will take you farther than you want to go, keep you longer than you want to stay, and cost you more than you want to pay." – Ravi Zacharias, Christian Apologist

PREFACE TO THE FALL OF MANKIND

Genesis 3 is an incredibly important chapter in the Bible, for without it, we would have no Bible as we know it. All of Scripture from this point forward, until the last two chapters of the Bible, deal with the consequences of sin and God's plan of redemption as He is on mission to save mankind.

BEFORE WE TALK about what happened on Earth here, we need to talk about what happened in Heaven, and even before that, we need to understand what angels are. Let's take a moment to have an Angelology Crash Course and answer a few questions:

Q: When did God create them?

A: According to Job 38:4 – 7 angels were created prior to the third day of creation because they "sang for joy" when God "laid the foundations of the Earth".

Q: How many angels did God create?

A: According to Revelation 5:11 & Hebrews 12:22, there are more than we can count; an "innumerable company".

Q: What is their purpose?

A: According to Hebrews 1:14, they were created to minister to those who would inherit salvation (Christians).

Q: What angels are named in the Bible?

A: There are four. 1) Gabriel (Daniel 8:16; Luke 1:19, 26), 2) Michael (Daniel 10:13, 21; 12:1; Jude 1:9; Revelation 12:7), 3) Abaddon (Revelation 9:11), and 4) Lucifer (Ezekiel 28:13 – 17; Isaiah 14:12 – 14)

NOW THAT WE'VE had an overview of Angels, let's have an overview of Satan, and how we got to this point in Genesis 3. We'll answer a few questions here too:

Q: What are his titles?

A: The Bible references him as "the dragon" (Revelation 12:3 – 9), "the devil" (John 8:44), the "serpent of old" (Revelation 20:2), "Lucifer" (Isaiah 14:12), "ruler of demons" (Matthew 12:24), "god of this world" (2nd Corinthians 4:4), "prince of the power of the air" (Ephesians 2:2), "accuser" (Matthew 4:1), "roaring lion" (1st Peter 5:8), "tempter" (Matthew 4:3), "the anointed Cherub" (Ezekiel 28:14), "Beelzebub" (Matthew 12:24), "Belial" (2nd Corinthians 6:15), "the wicked one" (Matthew 13:19) and "the adversary" which is often transliterated as "Satan" (Job 1 – 2)

Q: How is Satan described?

A: The two primary passages that describe Satan are Ezekiel 28:12 – 17 and Isaiah 14:12 – 15. At your convenience, take a moment to read those passages.

Q: How did Satan fall?

A: When compiling our Biblical data, here is what we get. Satan was created prior to the third day of creation as perfect and wise until pride began to stir in him (Job 38:4 – 7; Ezekiel 28:12 – 17). Satan then attempted to rise up against God by saying, "I will ascend into heaven, I will exalt my throne above the stars [angels] of God, I will also sit on the mount of the congregation on the farthest sides of the North, I will ascend above the heights of the clouds, and I will be like the Most High" (Isaiah 14:12 – 15). We can almost see that at the moment Satan said, "I will be like the Most High" that a war broke out in Heaven and Satan was cast down like lightning along with a third of the angels which are now called demons (Revelation 12:2 – 9; Luke 10:18).

THIS FORMERLY SHINING angel of Heaven has now become the darkened demon who has been terrorizing Earth since Genesis 3 in the Garden of Eden.

SATAN IN THE GARDEN

"the serpent" – This is the Hebrew word *nachash* which occurs 30x in the Old Testament and the definition refers to the modern taxonomy of a snake; however, as we will see, the snakes of today look different than in the Garden of Eden. Something to note is that the first sin and fall in existence occurred not in the physical realm, but the spiritual realm. Satan is trying to take down humanity with him.

"Has God indeed said…" – This is the first tactic of the enemy! Satan will do whatever he can to get you to question the authority of God and His word. This is why it is so important for you to have a strong understanding about the reliability of the Bible, worship God with your mind, and live out 1st Peter 3:15.

"'You shall not eat of every tree of the garden.?'" – The emphasis is on Satan's use of the word "every" as if to imply, "If

God *really* loved you, wouldn't He give you *everything*? Why would God hold something back from you?". Don't fall into the trap of Satan thinking God is holding out on you. Everything He says and does is to protect and promote your joy.

"... the woman said to the serpent..." – It is one thing for Satan to talk to Eve, but why did she respond back?! The Christian must never converse or negotiate with the enemy, but only rebuke and cast away demons in the name of Jesus (Jude 1:9)

I want you to take a moment to read and compare Genesis 2:16 – 17 with Genesis 3:2 – 3. Notice a few things here. Eve omitted the word "freely", added the phrase "nor shall you touch it", and failed to say that God "commanded" them to obey. Eve copied the devil further when she spoke of "God (*Elohim*) instead of "the LORD God"; His exclusive name. Finally, she said, "lest you die" which is a possibility, instead of "you shall surely die" which is an actuality. Eve took from, added to, and changed God's word. This was her first step to sin; not staying true to God's word. My friend, do not fall into the same trap Eve did. Know the Scriptures. Your life depends on it.

"'You will not surely die...'" – Notice what Satan does; he contradicts the truthfulness of God's word. Subtly, Satan is asserting himself as a higher authority and more truthful than God Himself. Satan just told Eve that God is a liar. You know, we're not much better at times. Every moment that we sin willfully, we are saying in our actions, "God is not in authority over my life, I am in authority over my life." If God is reminding you of areas of your life in which you're doing this, then make note of that, and start making practical steps to make things right.

"... you will be like God ..." – This is Satan's final deceptive statement. This is what Satan deceived himself with in Isaiah 14:14. Satan uses the same lies and tactics that he used in the Garden of Eden that he uses today; making people think they can be the god of their own life.

CHRIST IN GENESIS

Before we leave this very important chapter, I want us to see Christ in the midst of all of this:

- Thorns came from sin and Jesus wore them in John 19.
- Sin brought sweat and Jesus sweat great drops of blood as He was about to be murdered for us (Luke 22:44).
- Sin brought pain and suffering; the very thing Jesus went through for you (Matthew 27).
- Adam had a miraculous beginning just as Jesus had a miraculous beginning (Matthew 1:20 - 23).
- Adam was created perfect, innocent, and holy just as Jesus is. (Hebrews 7:26)
- Adam is the head of all humanity while Jesus is the head of all those in humanity that would be saved (Ephesians 5:23).
- Adam, representing mankind, was given dominion over the world, but Christ, who was raised from the dead is now seated at the right hand of the Father and has dominion over all things (1st Corinthians 15:27).
- Adam was put in a deep sleep and awoke to receive his bride. Christ, who "slept" in death ("to sleep" is the New Testament way to say a Christian died for in reality they die on Earth, but now are awakened in the presence of God in Heaven) is now receiving His Bride, the Church, to Himself (Revelation 19:6 - 8).
- Adam was tested by Satan and failed while Jesus was tempted by Satan and was victorious (Matthew 4).
- Adam, through his disobedience brought mankind death, while Jesus, through His obedience, now gives mankind the opportunity to have eternal life (Romans 5:12 - 21).

THIS CHAPTER IS the reason we see so much sin and suffering within us and within the world today. Yet, even in the darkest chapter of the Bible, God still shines His light and gives us hope. It's time for us to carry that hope into our dark and dying world. It's time to bring Jesus to lost people instead of waiting for them to come to us.

LET'S PRAY, *"Dear God, my heart is overwhelmed and heavy for how much sin and suffering I see around me. I can't even imagine how Your heart aches over Your creation. I know that in and of myself I can't do much, but in and through You nothing is impossible. Help me not fall into the same trap Adam and Eve did. Help me to know the truth of Your word so I'm not deceived by the lies of the enemy. As I walk in truth, help me to bring others with me. I ask this in the name of Jesus. Amen."*

ACTION POINT

We discussed earlier about how the first recorded tactic of the enemy is to get us to doubt the word of God. Therefore, we need to combat against this practically by knowing how the Bible is reliable so we can read it with confidence. With that being said, I want to give you a free copy of one of my books discussing this very topic. Simply email me at sean_arviso@yahoo.com and say, "I would like my free copy of Fact or Fiction." In addition to the content there, I included two and a half pages of resources at the end to go deeper. I also strongly recommend exploring the websites I shared with you at the end of Day Two and research specifically with regard to the reliability of the Bible. There are also lots of great podcasts that have plenty of free, but quality, content regarding this.

LEARN TO LOVE CHRISTIAN APOLOGETICS. Learn to love how you know the Bible is truly God's word. People will ask you questions regarding this. How will you answer?

DAY SIX

GENESIS 4:1 - 5:32

"The story of Cain and Abel, while in every way to be understood as actual history, is also a parable of the age-long conflict of the two seeds. Cain typifies the 'seed of the serpent' while Abel is a type of Christ, the 'seed of the woman.'" – Dr. Henry M. Morris, considered the father of modern Creation Science (1918 - 2006)

CAIN AND ABEL

From this point forward through the Old Testament, the New Testament, the past 2,000 years, to today, and until the events of Revelation 20, we will see mankind take one of two roads (Matthew 7:13 – 14). Everyone must make a choice; either walk the way of Cain or walk the way of Abel. We will now see Cain take center stage.

"... Adam knew Eve... " - The word "knew" is the Hebrew word *yada* which is used 974x throughout the Old Testament which means to know by experience. This will be the biblical euphemism used throughout Scripture to articulate sexual relations.

"… she conceived and bore Cain …" – The name "Cain" is the Hebrew word *qayin* which means possession, gotten, or acquire. Now, before we proceed, we need to remove our pre-conceived ideas or biases. Remember, both Cain and Abel are sinners in need of redemption.

"Then she bore again, this time his brother Abel." – The Hebrew word for Abel is *hebel* which is used 73x in the Old Testament and means breath or vapor. Throughout the book of Ecclesiastes we see this word *hebel* translated as vanity which brings up this interesting point. Cain's name reminds us that life comes from God and Abel's name reminds us that life is very brief; only a vapor and a breadth. Abel is the beginning of many shepherds who would come after him such as Abraham, Isaac, Jacob, the 12 sons of Jacob, Moses, and David. Of course, all of these shepherds are merely a shadow of the ultimate Shepherd, our Good Shepherd who is Jesus.

"And in the process of time…" – This is to show that their offerings unto the LORD were a continual practice; however, this time, something was different.

Why did God receive Abel's offering and not Cain's? Let's look at Abel's first. God made the first sacrifice of blood; thus, Abel is doing what he knows God will accept. Why did God honor this? Well, Hebrews 11:4 says, "by faith Abel offered a more excellent offering than Cain…" It was done in faith, and without faith, it is impossible to please God (Hebrews 11:6).

Now, let's look at Cain's offering. First, what does the New Testament say about Cain? 1st John 3:11 – 12, "For this is the message that you heard from the beginning, that we should love one another, not as Cain who was of the wicked one and murdered his brother. And why did he murder him? Because his works were evil and his brother's righteous." Jude 1:10 – 11, "But these [apostates] speak evil of whatever they do not know; and whatever they know naturally, like brute beasts, in these things they corrupt themselves. Woe to them! For they have gone in the way of Cain..." Remember, the best Bible Commentary is the Bible itself. So, why did God reject Cain's offering? It was not done in faith, not a blood sacrifice, not the first fruits, and there was a continual unrepentant wickedness in Cain's heart that was the real problem.

Notice something. Cain still gave a sacrifice. He still gave an offering to God. Though, in this context, it was not what God wanted, there are many in our churches today who don't give any sacrifices or offerings to the LORD at all! This begs the question: How much, if at all, do you and I sacrifice and offer? Listen friend. Whether you go down into the well, or you hold the rope for those who go down, either way, there should be scars on your hand. Are you the one going down into the well by doing hands-on ministry or are you the one holding the rope by giving financial, prayer, and other types of support? Where are your scars?

"And Cain was very angry, and his countenance fell." – The Hebrew word for "very" is *maod* which means exceedingly or with much force. The Hebrew word for "angry" is *charah* which means to burn hot with anger. He really lost it! You are now seeing pride rush from a man and consume him with rage. Remember, it wasn't for external reasons alone God rejected his offering, but for internal reasons; his heart wasn't right.

"So the LORD said to Cain..." – God actually spoke to him! Why didn't He just strike down Cain dead? What God is doing here is the same thing He does today; He is pursuing bitter and angry people with His love. Remember, there's a little bit of Cain in all of us at times. Yet, He still loves you.

"If you do well, will you not be accepted?" – Certainly, God is the God of 2nd chances. The LORD, after not killing him, was offering another chance to repent of his ways, to put away wrath, and be restored to his Maker. How beautiful it is that the moment we mess up and sin, God is right there ready to pick us up if we let Him.

"And if you do not do well, sin lies at the door." – This is the first mention of the word "sin" in the Bible. This is the Hebrew word *chatta'ath* which is used 296x in the Old Testament. Just as quickly as God gave the solution, He also gave the warning. Sin is always right around the corner and temptation will find you wherever you are. Here are several references I encourage you memorize and hide in your heart that you might not sin against God (Psalm 119:11): Galatians 2:20; Ephesians 6:10 – 20; 1st Corinthians 9:27; 2nd Corinthians 10:4 – 6; Philippians 4:8 – 9; Romans 8:1.

"And its desire is for you, but you should rule over it." – God is not only commanding what is right, but He is telling Cain that what is right is also possible. Remember, as a Christian, we are not fighting *for* victory, but we are fighting *from* victory. The instruction of God's word, the example Jesus, and the power of the Holy Spirit makes it possible for you to rule over sin instead of being ruled by it.

"Now Cain talked with Abel his brother..." – Jesus says in Luke 11:49 – 51 that Abel was the first prophet, which, by definition, is simply someone who speaks truth. No doubt Abel was speaking the truth of God trying to reason with his brother Cain to repent. Let this be a word for you if you have hostile family members towards the Gospel; love them and reason with them.

"... Cain rose up against Abel his brother and killed him." – This is the first murder and human death in the Bible. Anger, as we know, is a very powerful emotion. Every year angry drivers cause accidents that kill about 28,000 people on the U.S. highways. Angry people who have been fired from their jobs have killed innocent people as a form of retaliation. Many school shootings that occur in the U.S. are because a student was angry. So how do we begin countering this behavior? Romans 2:4 says that it is God's kindness that leads people to repentance, even the angry ones. The Church needs to be trained in loving angry people into the Kingdom of God.

"Then the LORD said to Cain..." – Wow. The patience of God. He is offering Cain *another* chance! Notice how God is always the one who comes to us first; He takes the initiative. Here are three passages that show God is still taking initiative today to reach lost people. 2nd Peter 3:9 says that God wants everyone to repent that they would not perish. John 6:44 says that He is the one drawing us to Himself. John 16:7 – 14 says that the Father is drawing us to Jesus to be saved, by the Holy Spirit.

"He said, 'I do not know. Am I my brother's keeper?'" – I don't know about you, but I would have probably killed Cain right there. What arrogance! Cain is the first murderer of all mankind and he has the audacity to lie sarcastically to God's face. I pray that the more you spend time in God's word you see just how gracious He truly is; both in the Old Testament as well as the New Testament.

"And Cain said to the LORD..." When you read Cain's response you notice that He is remorseful, but not repentant. Cain was concerned about his punishment and not about his character. Once again, we can't be too hard on Cain because sometimes we sin, we get caught, we suffer the consequences, but we're more concerned with what happened to us instead of how we sinned against God.

"And the LORD set a mark on Cain..." – God, who is rich in mercy (Ephesians 2:4) puts a mark on Cain to PROTECT him! Isn't it good that God didn't treat Cain like Cain treated Abel? Isn't it good that God doesn't treat you like you sometimes treat others?

LIFE PROMISED IN DEATH

Have you ever tried a Bible reading plan? If yes, how many times did you skip over the genealogies and long list of names (You can be honest!)? I want to show you something that hopefully changes your perspective on genealogies in the Bible. Genesis 5 is the first genealogy in the Bible and records 10 generations which span from Adam to Noah. We see the melancholy phrase "and he died" used 8x throughout this chapter. Death was now reigning over mankind because of Adam's sin (Romans 5:12 – 17, 21). It's important to note that in Hebrew culture, and much of Middle Eastern culture even today, names have significance. Names were given to represent something about the person's character, identify the events around their birth, or prophesy something about the future. Within this chapter, some are obscure and difficult to translate into English, but overall, there is a clear prophetic message God is communicating to us through the names of these real people in history. Let me show you. On the left is the Hebrew name and on the right is the English translation of that name.

- HEBREW (ENGLISH)
  - Adam (Man)
  - Seth (Appointed)
  - Enosh (Mortal)
  - Cainan (Sorrow)
  - Mahalalel (The Blessed God)
  - Jared (Shall come down)
  - Enoch (Teaching)
  - Methuselah (His death shall bring)
  - Lamech (The Despairing)
  - Noah (Rest / Comfort)

HERE'S what God is showing us: Mankind is mortal, dying, and sorrowful by being drenched in our sins, but the blessed God shall come down teaching and His death shall bring us, the despairing, rest and comfort. Do you see Jesus in this? Do you see the Gospel message? Genesis 5 is a prophecy embedded within the list of names. Genesis 5 is a chapter not just filled with death; it is God promising life in the midst of death. Even in the midst of darkness, God had a plan. Today, in your darkness, God still has a plan.

LET'S PRAY, *"Dear God, I am absolutely amazed at who You are. Thank You for being patient with me like You were patient with Cain. Thank You for constantly pursuing me even when I go against You and disobey You. Thank You for never giving up on me. Help me to have Your compassion and passionate action to reach those who've walked away from You. Please use me to bring people into fellowship with You and Your people. Please empower by Your Holy Spirit to do Your will. I ask this in the name of Jesus. Amen."*

ACTION POINT

Here is your Action Point for today: Reach out to someone you know personally that is going in the way of Cain, someone who used to go to church or have a relationship with God, but has now walked away from Him. Write down their name, pray for them consistently, fast for them, and make an effort today to start bringing that person back into fellowship with God and His people. Every situation is slightly different, so I also encourage you to contact your church leadership for prayer and wise counsel on the practical steps you should take.

IF YOU DON'T FIGHT for this person, who will?

DAY SEVEN

GENESIS 6:1 - 8:22

"For a hundred and twenty years the wits laughed, and the 'common sense' people wondered, and the patient saint went on hammering and pitching at his ark. But one morning it began to rain; and by degrees, somehow, Noah did not seem quite such a fool. The jests would look rather different when the water was up to the knees of the jesters; and their sarcasms would stick in their throats as they drowned. So is it always. So it will be at the last great day. The men who lived for the future, by faith in Christ, will be found out to have been the wise men when the future has become the present, and the present has become the past, and is gone forever; while they who had no aims beyond the things of time, which are now sunk beneath the dreary horizon, will awake too late to the conviction that they are outside the ark of safety, and that their epitaph is, 'Thou fool'". - Alexander Maclaren, Pastor & Author (1826 - 1910)

THE PROBLEM OF EVIL

The days of Noah were consumed with worldwide wickedness and violence. We look around today, see on the news, and experience daily the results of evil and some ask, "If God is so good and powerful, why is this happening?" I want to share with you that the problem of evil is actually evidence for the existence of God.

Let me explain. What is cold? It is the absence of heat. What is darkness? It is the absence of light. What is evil? It is the absence of good; ultimately, evil is the absence of God. The atheist cannot say, "That's wrong!" because whose standard of morality are they using? If it is their own, then anyone can claim to be the standard, and if it is God, then their atheism is a false belief system. To claim something is wrong is to have a moral understanding of what is right; whether you believe that originates from the God of the Bible or not.

NOAH THE RIGHTEOUS

"Noah found grace in the eyes of the LORD." – This is the first mention of the word grace in the Bible. Everyone who has ever been saved from the punishment of their sin has been saved by grace, through faith. No one has been saved by bringing a sacrifice (Hebrews 10:1 – 4), keeping the law (Galatians 2:16), or good works (Isaiah 64:6). Like Noah, we must all find grace in God's eyes. How do we do that? Not by trusting in our unsatisfactory work, but in the satisfactory work of Christ on the cross.

"… Noah was a just man, perfect…" – The Hebrew word for "just" is *tsaddiyq* which means righteous. The Hebrew word for "perfect" is *tamiym* which means complete, with integrity, or blameless. This is the first mention of the word righteous and Noah's righteousness is mentioned in Ezekiel 14:14, 20; Hebrews 11:7; 2nd Peter 2:5. Noah must've learned the ways of God from his father Lamech, who learned from his father Methuselah, who learned from his father Enoch. Whether you have kids or not, this raises the question, "Who am I discipling?"

It can be said that righteous describes Noah's standing before God and blameless describes Noah's standing before people. If you haven't seen it yet, Noah's life is a major rebuke to us. Many of us think the Christian life is difficult because of wordly influences around us, or we wish we had more Christian friends and family. Listen. Noah was walking with God when literally NO ONE was walking with God out of the billions alive on the Earth with the arguable exception of his 7 closest family members. Noah's life challenges me to live righteously before God and blameless before others. I hope he challenges you too.

CONSTRUCTION OF THE ARK

"... cubit..." – This is the Hebrew word *ammah* which is a Hebrew measurement from your elbow to your fingertips. The average cubit would equate to 18 inches. Therefore, the ark was 450ft long (1 ½ football fields), 75ft wide, and 45ft high. God gave Noah the blueprint to the first ship ever constructed and all ships after would follow the same 6 to 1 ratio; length being 6x the width. Because there were 3 levels within this vessel, there would have been over 1,500,000 cubic feet worth of space. Because only the "kinds" and not the "species" of land and air animals needed to go on the Ark, and they would not have all likely been fully grown, there would have been plenty of room for the animals, Noah's family, and supplies for the journey. I highly recommend a book called Noah's Ark: A Feasibility Study by John Woodmorappe if you want technical information for how these events were in reality.

"Thus Noah did; according to all that God commanded him..." – A great example for us today. Noah did not complain about the

120 year task, he simply obeyed and trust that God was going to provide the resources, ability, strength, and wisdom to accomplish what he was told to do. Hold onto this truth: Where God quides, God provides.

A quick note regarding Noah's work-ethic. Not only was this a pioneering effort, it was undoubtedly a back-breaking effort. All throughout the Bible work is seen as a command and a blessing (Proverbs 6:6 – 11; 12:24; 13:4; 14:23; Ephesians 4:28; 1st Timothy 5:8; 1st Thessalonians 4:11 – 12; 2nd Thessalonians 3:10 – 12). For a Christian to be called lazy, not punctual, or procrastinating is shameful to the name of Christ. Let's be men and women who not only work hard, but with integrity, and for the glory of God.

GLOBAL CATASTROPHE

It was just another day. People were walking, working, eating, sleeping, kids outside playing, friends laughing with each other, and then something happened that had never happened before; rain. As the drops of water began to fall, the bewilderment of mankind quickly turned into a terrified worldwide panic. The Earth shook, water fell heavily from the sky for 40 days and the ground broke as water forcefully burst upward continually until God commanded the water to stop. From the Ark you could hear shrieks of fear as people swam for their life to the boat or clung to each other in a desperate attempt to survive. Days passed and the Earth was now silent. Billions dead. No one expected this. Remember, God loves every single one of them, but He is also a God of justice.

These events are real. However, they are also prophetic of the days you live in right now. Jesus says in Luke 17:26 – 27, "And as it was in the days of Noah, so it will be also in the days of the Son of Man: They ate, they drank, they married wives, they were given in marriage, until the day that Noah entered the ark, and the flood came and destroyed them all." At the time the Church is raptured, God's judgment will begin to fall upon the Earth during the 7 year Tribulation Period and then ultimately at the Great White Throne Judgment (Revelation 20).

Jesus says in Luke 12:48, "to whom much is given, from him much will be required". As your knowledge of Scripture increases, so does your responsibility to preach the Gospel. So, who are you trying to bring upon the Ark to be saved from God's wrath?

BIBLICAL NUMEROLOGY

As you read and study the Bible I want you to understand something interesting. Biblical Numerology is the study of numbers in the Bible having significance and symbolism. This is debated in many Christian circles, but something worth thinking about:

- 1 – The Number of Unity (Deuteronomy 6:4).
- 2 – The Number of Division. Jesus has two natures; human and divine. There are two testaments; old & new. Mankind is male and female. There are two types of people; saints and aint's (Christians and non-Christians).
- 3 – The Number of Completion *Connected with 7 & 10*. The Trinity is Father, Son, and Holy Spirit. The Universe is time, space, and matter. You are a body, soul, and spirit. Both the Tabernacle and Temple had three parts: the court, the holy place, and the sanctuary.
- 4 – The Number of Creation. North, East, South, and West. There are four seasons.
- 5 – The Number of Grace. The Holy Anointing Oil (Representative of the Holy Spirit) was pure and composed of 5 parts (Exodus 30:23 – 25)

- 6 – The Number of Man. Man was created on the 6th day. Man is supposed to labor for 6 days. The 6th commandment is not to murder.
- 7 – The Number of Completion. 7 days in a week. There 7 seal, 7 trumpet, and 7 bowl judgments in Revelation administered by 7 angels. 7 parables in Matthew. 7 "eternals" in Hebrews: "A priest forever" (1:6), "eternal salvation" (1:9), "eternal judgment" (6:2), "eternal redemption" (9:12), "eternal spirit" (9:14), "eternal inheritance" (9:15), "and everlasting covenant" (13:20). Jesus said 7 things on the cross.
- 8 – The Number of New Beginnings. 8 people on Noah's Ark in the 8th chapter of the Bible. Circumcision was commanded to be on the 8th day of life.
- 9 – The Number of Judgment. There are 9 Greek words for judgment derived from the Greek word *dikay*.
- 10 – The Number of Completion There are 10 commandments. 1/10 of your income is a tithe. There were 10 plagues against Egypt.
- 12 – The Number of Government. There were 12 tribes of Israel. 12 Apostles. The Heavenly Jerusalem has 12 foundations, 12 gates, 12 pearls, and 12 angels.
- 40 – The Number of Trials. It rained for 40 days during Noah's Flood. The Israelites wandered for 40 years. Moses was on the mountain with God for 40 days. Jonah was at Ninevah for 40 days. Jesus was tempted for 40 days.

THERE ARE many more we could cover, but we'll stop there. Here's what I want us to see. Here in the 8th chapter of Genesis, God is going to use 8 people to bring about a new beginning for mankind. This is where God makes it personal for us. One day, after you've gone through the wilderness of this life as a pilgrim, as God's ambassador of His Kingdom, you will rest with Him in Heaven forever. How did you get there? He carried you from this life into the next on the Ark of Salvation, Jesus Christ.

LET'S PRAY, *"Dear God, I feel speechless. Sin brings death and suffering. Help me to really believe that to where it causes me to be nauseated at the thought of sinning against You and others. Break my heart for what breaks Yours. Help me to see my community the way You do. Help me to bring lost people to Jesus, the Ark of salvation. Help me to be like Noah who was righteous before You and blameless before others. Use me Lord. Here I am at Your service. I ask this in the name of Jesus. Amen."*

ACTION POINT

Our world is dying. People are hurting. People are lost. More unfortunate and important is that people are under the wrath of God because of their sin. With that being said, here is your Action Point for today: Learn how to share the Gospel. Let me give you some resources that you can research online to get started:

- Romans Road to Salvation
- Gospel Colors
- The Way of the Master

I STRONGLY ENCOURAGE you to talk with your church leadership about two things: 1) How are they teaching people to evangelize and 2) how are they actively going out and evangelizing? In addition to learning an evangelism technique, it's important to be able to communicate your testimony of how God saved you.

LET's work together to bring lost people onto the Ark of salvation before it's too late.

DAY EIGHT

GENESIS 9:1 - 11:32

"Some wish to live within the sound of church and chapel bell. I want to run a rescue shop within a yard of hell!" - Charles Thomas Studd, British Missionary to China, India, & Africa (1860 - 1931)

YOU ARE CALLED to be a missionary. To answer God's call on your life by bringing the Gospel to the world, beginning with your community, is to be on the front lines of Kingdom work where life and death, sin and grace, Heaven and Hell converge. In today's reading of Genesis we have seen the origin of the nations. How are you and your local church reaching the nations with the Good News of Jesus?

7 COVENANTS IN THE BIBLE

Genesis 6:18 is the first mention of the word "covenant" and we see the word again here in Genesis 9:9 where God gives the rainbow as a sign of the Noahic Covenant. "Covenant" comes from the Hebrew word *beriyth* which means an agreement between two or more parties. Conditional covenants are based on the condition of man's performance and unconditional are agreements that God will accomplish regardless of mankind's performance. The word covenant is used 284x throughout the Old Testament and it's important we briefly see the 7 Covenants of the Bible:

The Eternal Covenant - The Father and the Son made an agreement regarding the elect. This covenant was made before the universe was created, and it consisted of the Father promising to bring to the Son all whom the Father had given Him (John 6:39; 17:9, 24). Son would become man (Col. 2:9; 1 Tim. 2:5), become for a while lower than the angels (Heb. 2:7), and be found under the Law (Gal. 4:4-5). The Son would die for the sins of the world (1 John 2:2; 1 Pet. 2:24), and the Father would raise the Son from the Dead (Psalm 2). Where the Eternal Covenant was made between the Father and the Son, the New Covenant is made between God and Man.

The Adamic Covenant (Conditional) – This was a covenant made by God and Adam where Adam would have everlasting life based upon obedience to God. This was possible because Adam had no sin nature (Gen. 2:16 – 17). The promise connected to that covenant was life, the condition was perfect obedience, and the penalty was death.

The Noahic Covenant (Unconditional) – This was God's promise to Noah, the animals, and the Earth to never again destroy the world with a flood. God gave the rainbow as a sign (Gen. 9:8 – 17).

The Abrahamic Covenant (Unconditional) – There were three main features: 1) The promise of land (Gen. 15:18 – 21; Deut. 30:1 – 10), 2) the promise of descendants (Gen. 12:4; 17:6) , and 3) the promise of blessing and redemption (Amplified under the New Covenant).

The Mosaic Covenant or The Old Covenant (Conditional) –

The blessings that God promised Israel under the Old Covenant were predicted upon their obedience to the Mosaic Law. The sacrificial system under the Mosaic Law did not take away sins (Heb. 10:1 – 4), but was to foreshadow the Lamb of God who would take away the sins of the world (Gal. 3:23 – 25; Heb. 9:11 – 28).

The Davidic Covenant (Unconditional) – God promises to David through the prophet Nathan (2nd Sam. 7; 1st Chron. 17:11 – 14; 2nd Chron. 6:16) that the Messiah would come through his lineage and the tribe of Judah. This is unconditional because God does not place any conditions on its fulfillment.

The New Covenant or the Covenant of Grace (Unconditional) – This is that gracious, undeserved, agreement between the offended God and the offending sinner in which God promises salvation and eternal life to all those who put their faith in Christ (Eph. 2:8 – 9; Jn. 3:16 – 17; Rom. 10:9 – 10). The New Covenant was promised in Eden (Gen. 3:15), it was proclaimed to Abraham (Gen. 12:3), and it was fulfilled in Christ (Lk. 1:67 – 79).

THE NATIONS OF THE WORLD

Genesis 10 is known as the Table of Nations. The purpose of this chapter is found in Genesis 10:1, 32 which was to give a record of the Earth's repopulation from the three sons of Noah after the Flood. It's important to be aware of three things with regard to Genesis 10. Firstly, this is not a typical genealogy which gives only the names of descendants. We see that all of these names represent many more nations, languages, and territories. We are seeing the movement of people and nations in the ancient world. Secondly, this listing is not complete. For example, we don't find Edom, Moab, and Ammon mentioned even though they are very important in Biblical history. Thirdly, it's difficult to identify some of these nations and give them modern names. Over the many centuries nations change their names, move locations, modify language, and even alter their ethnic composition through intermarriage.

There are also three important points with regard to the nations of the world. Firstly, all nations originate from one race and bloodline (Acts 17:26). Though one people group may be more advanced economically, politically, technologically, etc. that does not mean one people group has more value than another. The result of this truth should be the extinguishment of racism (Philippians 2:3 – 4). Secondly, the plan of redemption is for all humanity. We are all one blood and have one need; the Savior through the line of Shem, the line of David, and the virgin birth of Mary; Jesus Christ. Frequently in the book of Psalms you find the phrase, "all you lands" or "all nations" (Psalm 67). The Old Testament, and not just the New Testament, expresses God's desire to see the nations be restored to their Creator. Thirdly, all nations leave a legacy. A nation is obviously comprised of people, but more specifically, many individuals. What you believe determines what you think, what you think determines what you do, what you do determines your habits, your habits determine your lifestyle, and your lifestyle determines your legacy. Therefore, to study the nations of the Earth past and present is to study the beliefs, thoughts, actions, habits, and lifestyle of that nation which left behind their legacy. What do you want your country's legacy to be? What do you want your legacy to be?

TOWER OF BABEL

In Genesis 11:1 we see the word "language" which is the Hebrew word *saphah*, used 176x in the Old Testament, which means lip. "Speech" is the Hebrew word *dabar*, used 1,439x in the Old Testament, which means word, speaking, or utterance. It's important to note something at this time. In Hebrew literature (Which the Bible was written entirely by Hebrews except for the Gospel of Luke and the Book of Acts), whenever a writer wanted to emphasize something, they repeated it. Moses' usage of the words *saphah* and *dabar* is to give repetition to emphasize that there was only one language and speech throughout the entire world. People have speculated that this language was some form of ancient Hebrew or perhaps related to Old Akkadian, but no one knows definitively.

The result of God's intervention was the birth of a variety of languages and dialects; thus, giving rise to etymology and linguistics. According to the Linguistic Society of America and their study in 2009, there are 6,909 distinct languages. According to Wycliffe, a Bible Translation organization, only about 670 languages have the entire Bible translated. This is a great accomplishment, but there is still a great amount of work to be done to get God's whole word to the whole world.

Once again, this is all an act of God's grace. He could have wiped them all out for their disobedience, but instead provided a way out and ultimately another opportunity to repent. How beautiful it is that God doesn't wipe us out when we disobey, but instead continues providing opportunities for us to repent and be restored to Him.

SHEM

First of all, why are the list of names in Genesis 11:10 – 32, and other genealogies in the Bible, important? Well, what to us may seem like a menial list of names is really a bridge. This bridge of people throughout history, from Adam to the Messiah, shows us God's faithfulness to the world by keeping His promise to provide a Savior. In Genesis 9:26 – 27 we find an amazing prophecy concerning Shem. Noah gave glory to God for what He was about to do with the descendants of Shem. It was through Shem that Terah, Abraham, Isaac, Jacob, Jesse, David, and ultimately the Messiah would come. Though Shem was Noah's second-born (Gen. 9:24; 10:21), whenever the three sons are mentioned, Shem is always first even though, culturally, the first-born would be named first. This is another example of God, in His grace, elevating the second-born in place of the first-born. God chose Abel instead of Cain (Gen. 4:4 – 5), Abraham instead of Haran (Gen. 11:26), Isaac instead of Ishmael (Gen. 17:15 – 22), Jacob instead of Esau (Gen. 25:19 – 23), and King David, who was not the first king, over Saul, who was (Ps. 89:20 – 29). These are Old Testament historical examples of a New Testament spiritual truth; that you must be born-again (Jn. 3:3). God does not honor your first birth of the flesh; He honors your second birth of the Spirit. This, Jesus says, is what grants you permission into the Kingdom.

If Genesis 1 – 11 is a record of 4 key events: Creation, The Fall, The Flood, and The Judgment at Babel, then Genesis 12 – 50 is the record of 4 key men: Abraham, Isaac, Jacob, and Joseph. We will discuss this in more detail as we continue our 30-Day In His Presence Challenge together through the Book of Genesis.

LET'S PRAY, *"Dear God, I'm amazed at Your care for the world. It's difficult for me to unconditionally love a few people while You unconditionally love all people. Help me to love everyone like You do. Help me to be a part of Your global mission in reaching the lost. Please use me and my local church to take Your whole word to the whole world. I ask this in the name of Jesus. Amen."*

ACTION POINT

Today we discussed God's love for the nations of the world, and specifically, people groups who do not yet have an entire Bible or any Scripture in their language. Here is your Action Point for today: Contact your local church and see what they are doing in regard to Global Mission work; specifically in the area of Bible

Translation. Pray for the work of Bible Translators and these people groups who do not yet have God's word in their language. Ask the Lord how He wants you to partner with your local church in Global Missions and Bible Translation efforts. God, through the Church worldwide, has done a great work, but there is still much more work to be done until He calls us home. So let's get to it.

DAY NINE

GENESIS 12:1 - 14:24

"Abraham's journey was long and challenging; he worked hard and experienced both grief and blessings. Most of the time, he couldn't see the path ahead, but he held strong to the promise in his heart. God would continue to fulfill that promise over a thousand years after Abraham's death until its completion in Jesus Christ." - Liz Kanoy, Senior Editor of Crosswalk.com

ABRAM

Abram, whose name means "exalted father", would later have his name changed by God to Abraham (Gen. 17:5) which means, "father of many nations". He is not only important in the Old Testament, but important in the New Testament being mentioned 67x. He is patriarch to the 3 major monotheistic religions in the world which are Judaism, Christianity, and Islam. Like all of God's people Abram had his successes and failures, both of which we can learn from thousands of years later. Let's look at the calling of Abram, his blunder in Egypt, and his faith.

Firstly, when God called Abram, he was already 75 years old! This clearly shows age is no limitation or obstacle for God and He can truly use anyone who is willing. When God called Abram, him and Sarai were childless. This would precursor God providing their miracle baby and prove He can do the impossible. When God called Abram, he was still a pagan (Josh. 24:2)! This is an Old Testament example of a New Testament truth when Jesus says, "You have not chosen Me, but I have chosen you." (Jn. 15:16). Secondly, how God called Abram, the Bible tells us God appeared (Acts 7:2) and spoke (Gen. 12:1) to Abram. This is another Old Testament example of a New Testament truth that faith comes by hearing the word of God (Rom. 10:17). Thirdly, why God called Abram, it was for at least three reasons: 1) God loved him and desired his salvation. 2) God purposed to use him to bless the whole world. 3) To use Abram as an example of what it means to walk by faith.

In today's reading we saw Abram experience the spiritual success of moving by faith to Canaan, but we also saw his spiritual failure by taking a detour to Egypt. We see at least four changes Abram went through in Egypt which examples of what NOT to do. Firstly, Abram moved from trusting to scheming. Instead of trusting God to stay in Canaan regardless of the circumstances, he schemed his own survival in Egypt. There was no altar and no place of worship for him; that was in Bethel ("Beth", which means house, and "El" which means God. "Bethel", therefore, means House of God). Abram and Sarai brought this half-truth from Ur (Gen. 20:13), used it in Egypt and Gerar (Gen. 12:10 – 20; Gen. 20), and then their son Isaac adopted it (Gen. 26). It should go without saying that, especially as a child of God, it is never good to lie your way out of trouble. One lie is only covered by another lie. Let truth unravel the web of lies you're trapped in so you can walk in freedom. Secondly, Abram moved from confidence to fear. The only fear we as Christians should have is the fear of the Lord (Ps. 111:10; Prov. 1:7; 8:13;

14:26 – 27; Eccl. 12:13; Matt. 10:28). We must learn from Abram what NOT to do by allowing our fear, reverence, respect, and worship of God to be overcome by any other potential fears of people or circumstances. Thirdly, Abram moved from others-minded to self-minded. When we read Genesis 12:10 – 20 we see Abram cared more about self-preservation than the protection of his wife Sarai. This is an important reminder for men in general to be defenders rather than cowards, but especially a reminder for husbands to lay down their lives for their spouse instead of using them for personal gain. Fourthly, Abram moved from bringing blessing to bringing judgment. God called Abram to be a blessing to the nations (Gen. 12:1 – 3), but because of his disobedience, judgment fell on Pharaoh and his household (Gen. 12:17). Do you want to be a blessing to those around you? If you answered yes, then be a blessing to God first by staying in His will.

It's important at this point to briefly discuss faith. The Bible describes faith for us in Hebrews 11:1, 6 and simply means "to lean your full weight upon. A person gets saved and becomes born-again when they lean the full weight of their soul upon Jesus for forgiveness and salvation. We walk by faith when we lean the full weight of our lives upon God and His word. There are three points of faith we see from Abram's life so far that have application to us. First, faith brings you out. Faith in God's word brought Abram out of his hometown Ur. In the same way, as we walk by faith, God will often remove us from our comfort zones to use us in greater ways. Second, faith brings you in. Faith in God's word brought Abram into Canaan, the land of promise. You and I have our own land of Canaan to enter and our own plans from God to walk into. Third, faith brings you on. Faith in God's word brought Abram on to new challenges as he was constantly moving (Gen. 12:4 – 9). Today, you and I are called to take up our cross (Matt. 16:24), live as pilgrims in the land (1st Pet. 2:11), and fight the good fight of faith (1st Tim. 6:12) as committed soldiers in His army (2nd Tim. 2:3). Remember this: comfortable Christianity is not biblical Christianity.

MELCHIZEDEK

In Genesis 14:18 – 24 we are introduced to a mysterious figure named Melchizedek whose name means "king of righteousness" from Salem, which means "peace". He is also recorded as a priest even though the Aaronic Priesthood would not be established for another 700 years! Melchizedek appears to have both governmental and spiritual authority. The fact that Melchizedek blessed Abraham shows that Melchizedek was clearly superior (Heb. 7:7). Genesis 14:19 – 20 is the only record of Melchizedek speaking and his words bless both God and Abram. The High Priest of Israel would later have the responsibility of representing the people to God and representing God to the people. Abram tithes to Melchizedek (First mention of tithing in the Bible) and is another indicator that Melchizedek is superior. Notice what Melchizedek brought out; bread and wine. What does this remind you of? Clearly there is more to this figure than an enigmatic mention and placement in history. I would like you to see that Melchizedek's life was not only a foreshadowing of the Messiah to come, but he is another example proving the reliability of the Bible.

After Melchizedek's encounter with Abram, he is not seen or mentioned for another 1,000 years until King David writes in Psalm 110:4, "You [Messiah] are a priest forever according to the order of Melchizedek." Psalm 110 is what's called a Messianic Psalm because it prophesies of the Savior to come. After this, we don't see Melchizedek mentioned for another 1,000 years until the writer of Hebrews uses his name 9x to reveal an amazing truth. Melchizedek, a real figure in history, was also typological or a foreshadow of the true King Priest named Jesus. I strongly encourage reading Hebrews 5:1 – 11; 6:19 – 7:27 to enjoy this further. This topic of Melchizedek is supporting evidence for the reliability of the Bible because you don't get a perplexing figure like Melchizedek spoken of by three different people, each separated by 1,000 years, whose accounts are in the same book being the Bible, and whose fulfillment is in the same person, Jesus Christ; unless, God divinely orchestrated it all.

It has been said that a wise person learns from their mistakes, but a wiser person learns from the mistakes of others. My prayer for you is not only that you learn from your own experiences, but also from the experiences of others, specifically, from the life of Abram.

LET'S PRAY, *"Dear God, thank You for Your word. In it I find real people with real problems. In Your word I find You using messed up people, just like Abram, just like me, for Your bigger plans and purposes. Please help me to learn my from own experiences, successes, and failures, as well as learning from others'. Please stretch me, mold me, refine me, and build me into the disciple You want me to be. I ask this in the name of Jesus. Amen"*

~

ACTION POINT

Earlier, from the life of Abram, we discussed how comfortable Christianity is not biblical Christianity. Today, your Action Point is to get uncomfortable: Talk to 3 of your closest Christian mentors, pastors, and/or friends and ask them to be completely honest when asking the following questions:

1) WHAT IN my life do you see is a waste of God's time and/or resources?

. . .

2) WHAT DO you think I should be doing differently, more of, or less of to be a better follower of Jesus?

3) BASED on our relationship and how well you know me, what do you think God is calling me to do in life, why do you say that, and what steps should I take to move forward in that direction?

GROWTH CANNOT OCCUR without challenge and challenge cannot occur without change. Start getting comfortable with being uncomfortable. It's biblical.

DAY TEN

GENESIS 15:1 - 17:27

"**M**y fear is that of all the choices people face today, the one they rarely consider is, 'How can I serve most effectively and fruitfully in the local church?' I wonder if the abundance of opportunities to explore today is doing less to help make well-rounded disciples of Christ and more to help Christians avoid long term responsibility and have less long-term impact." - Kevin DeYoung, Pastor & Author

THIS IS a good word from Kevin in light of what we've read in Genesis today, what we'll be discussing in today's devotional reading, and our Action Point.

ABRAHAMIC COVENANT

As you travel through Genesis, and really the Bible as a whole, try imagining yourself in the lives of these people. These are real people, with real emotions, in real places, in real events, and God really used them. Today we've seen some really bad decisions that God still used to be really good outcomes.

In Genesis 15:10, what Abram did is known as "cutting a covenant". This ritual contract involved the death of animals and the binding of people to a promise. The persons making the covenant would sacrifice several animals and divide the bodies, placing the halves opposite of the other. The two, or more, parties would then walk between the pieces of the sacrifices to publicly declare that, if they failed to keep their word, then they agreed to the same fate as the animals. Notice something though; only God passed through the animals (Genesis 15:17). Therefore, the Abrahamic Covenant is an unconditional covenant because it is only based upon God's performance and fulfilling His promise. This was certainly no light or laughing matter. In fact, if you want to see how seriously God takes cutting a covenant, or making a promise, read Jeremiah 34:8 – 22. Important truths like this ought to make me even more thankful of Jesus fulfilling the Law that I could not fulfill, be the perfect sacrifice, and allow me to live under the New Covenant of Grace. Thank God my salvation, my forgiveness, and my eternal life with Him is not based upon my work and performance, but solely upon His work and performance.

I would like to show you something interesting regarding Genesis 15:12 about Abram falling into a "deep sleep". We don't know exactly what this event looked like, but we do see another passage of foreshadowing here. Abram's deep sleep, just as Adam's deep sleep, foreshadowed the deep sleep, or the death of Christ, right before the glory to follow. After Adam's deep sleep, he had his bride. After Abram's deep sleep, God made an unconditional covenant with him. After Christ's deep sleep ("Sleep" is a New Testament euphemism communicating a Christian died), He resurrected, defeating death, and is now having a Bride brought to Him; the Bride of Christ, the Church (Rom. 6:4; 1st Cor. 15; 1st Thess. 4:14.)

HAGAR AND ISHMAEL

You could say Genesis 16 is the first episode of the Jerry Springer Show (If you know, you know). If anyone tells you the Bible is boring, they clearly don't know their Bible very well! In today's reading we see Abram and Sarai taking a painful detour from their walk of faith which resulted not only in conflict within the household, but conflict within the world. This is the beginning of the Arab-Israeli conflict. Before we move on, keep this in mind: There are no great men and women of God, there are only wicked sinners saved by a great and loving God. This is true for Abram, this is true for all of us.

In light of the drama we just read about between Abram, Sarai, and Hagar, I would like to give you the 7 Steps to Stupid Choices. This is what they followed, and if you want similar disastrous results, then simply follow these and you'll be well on your way:

1. Fear your circumstances – Sarai is looking at the outward circumstances, but not the spiritual circumstances. Here is an important Christian life principle: God never called you to understand everything, He simply called you to trust Him. Sarai let her fear of circumstances overcome her faith in God.

2. Misinterpret God's activity as inactivity – Sarai thinks that God isn't working; therefore, she feels the need to "help God" out" and intervene. Let me just say this: God is ALWAYS working and it is ALWAYS for your good. Never forget that. Now, if you've ever felt bitter because you think God isn't working how you think He should, then please hold tightly to this passage, Romans 8:28 – 29.

3. Rationalize sin – It was culturally acceptable and practiced during the era of these people to have numerous wives and/or have sex with another woman

in order for her to be a surrogate to the couple. Abram and Sarai basically looked around and said, "Well, everyone else is doing it!". Please. Do NOT look to your culture as the standard, look to God and His word as the standard. We must not seek to do what simply works, we must seek to do what is right.

4. Misdefine the promises of God – Notice what Sarai said, "… perhaps, I shall obtain children by her." She is subtly trying to fulfill the promise of God her way instead of waiting on God's timing. Don't be like a horse rushing ahead of God and don't be like a donkey digging your heels in refusing to go where He wants you to. Walk with Him.

5. Listen to the voice of man over the voice of God – Abram got talked into this by his wife. We don't know the state of his heart, but I don't imagine it was too hard for him to say yes to this. Let this serve as a reminder to be careful who you take advice from. Be on guard, even in your closest relationships.

6. Allow yourself to be under the pressure of time – Abram and Sarai have so far waited 10 years for the promise of God to be fulfilled. Some of us can't even wait 10 minutes for our coffee from the café! Do you know why their God-honoring integrity failed? Because patience failed.

7. Take action into your own hands – If you want yourself on a fast track to destruction then do whatever is right in your own eyes (Judg. 21:25; Prov. 3:7; 26:12).

THE ANGEL OF THE LORD

There is an important phrase found in Genesis 16:7 called "Angel of the LORD". This is both the first mention of the phrase and the word "angel" which comes from the Hebrew word *malak* and means messenger or representative. As we examine this phrase we find that it is a Christophany, or, a preincarnate appearance of Jesus, the 2nd Person of the Trinity. The following passages mention the "Angel of the LORD" which I encourage you to read along with its context: Genesis 16:13; 22:15 – 16; 31:11 – 13; 48:15 – 16; Exodus 3:2, 6; Judges 6:22 – 23; 13:18; Isaiah 9:6; Hosea 12:3 – 4. The Angel of the LORD is Jesus Christ preincarnate and is fulfilling the office of an angel, or a messenger. Hebrews 1:1 – 2 is an important passage with regard to this topic because the writer explains how God spoke at various times and in various ways, but in these last days has spoken to us by His Son. Jesus is the ultimate messenger or representative of God because He is in fact God in the flesh.

THE SIGN OF THE COVENANT

As we enter Genesis 17, Abram and Sarai have been waiting 24 years for God to fulfill His promise of providing a son. Why did God wait for Abram to be 100 years old to fulfill His promise (Gen. 17:1, 21)? So that Abram would be "as good as dead" (Heb. 11:12) and God would prove Himself to truly be the Almighty (Gen. 17:1). Why does God wait to move powerfully in your life? So that He can go above and beyond your expectations (Eph. 3:20) for your good and His glory.

The sign of the Abrahamic Covenant was circumcision. All descendants of Abraham became known as "the circumcision" (Acts 10:45) while all Gentiles were called "the uncircumcision" (Eph. 2:11). Over time, the term circumcision took on a variety of meanings. "Uncircumcised lips" (Ex. 6:12) signified a lack of skill in public speaking. "Uncircumcised ears" and "hearts" (Lev. 26:41; Deut. 10:16; 30:6; Jer. 6:10; Acts 7:51) spoke of failure to hear, love, and obey the LORD. "Uncircumcised in the flesh" (Ezek. 44:7) meant unclean. However, what does the New Testament say about circumcision? "In Him you were also circumcised with the circumcision made without hands, by putting off the body of the sins of the flesh, by the circumcision of Christ..." (Col. 2:11). How interesting.

God commanded that all male babies 8 days old be circumcised (Gen. 17:12 – 13). What is significant about the number 8? Check back to Day Seven when we discussed Biblical Numerology. The number 8 represents new beginnings. It's amazing that when Jewish males put off the flesh on the 8th day, they now have a new identity. It's amazing that when a person receives Christ and is born-again, they are made a new person with a new identity (2nd Cor. 5:17). The circumcision of Abraham was simply a shadow of the ultimate circumcision that Christ would bring to all those who receive him. The physical cutting off of the flesh was to represent what God wanted to do in our hearts and spiritually; cut off and put to death our old fleshly nature.

The fact that, in Christ, we are new people is something to constantly rejoice about! My prayer is that our rejoicing would not only be internal, but external. My desire is that our joy would overflow from words into actions. My hope is that we wouldn't sprint in our service to God and burn out, but rather, endure the race of faith together as a marathon (2nd Tim. 4:7; Heb. 12:1).

LET'S PRAY, *"Dear God, I know I still mess up. I know there are days when my old person, my flesh rises up and wins a battle, but thank You for winning the war over my soul. Thank You for circumcising my heart through Christ and the fact that my identity is found in the work of Jesus instead of the work of my sin. Help me to always sing, rejoice, and take joy in this truth so much so that it causes me to serve You more passionately. Thank You for always loving me. I ask this in the name of Jesus. Amen."*

ACTION POINT

Earlier we talked about the "7 Steps to Stupid Choices", but now, I want us to implement a simple Biblical principle specifically regarding you and your local church.

PSALM 37:4 teaches that if you delight yourself in the Lord, He will give you the desires of your heart. If you honestly love Jesus, love spending time with Him in prayer, love reading His word, and love what God loves, then your desires begin to supernaturally conform to His desires. Basically, love God and do whatever you want. This brings us to today's Action Point. Think about the local church you attend and ask yourself, "What would I love to do in my local church?" Perhaps you want to join an existing ministry or perhaps God is prompting you to start a new ministry. Talk to your church leadership about what area you can get involved with.

LET'S nurture a Christian culture of "I get to serve God" instead of "I have to serve God". If we really delight in Him, then we will not only stay away from the "7 Steps to Stupid Choices", but we will be making decisions that are pleasing to our Savior.

DAY ELEVEN

GENESIS 18:1 - 20:18

"Brethren, if we are to be the friends of God we must be copartners with Him. He gives over to us all that He has, and friendship with God will necessitate that we give to Him all that we have. It has been well said that if God is ours we cannot be poor, because God has all, and we have all in having God." - Charles Haddon Spurgeon, the "Prince of Preachers" (1834 - 1892)

FRIEND OF GOD

Several passages mention that Abraham was a "friend of God" (2nd Chronicles 20:7; Isaiah 41:8; James 2:23) and this truth is demonstrated in our passage today. Friendship involves ministry, or service, and today we saw in Genesis 18 Abraham serving the LORD, his family, and then a lost world.

In Genesis 18:1 – 8, Abraham ministered to the LORD in six ways. First, Abraham served personally. Here is a man with over 300 servants and could have easily commanded others to do this, but instead, he chooses to serve the LORD directly. Second, Abraham served immediately. Abraham could have been sleeping during the heat of the day which would have been customary for this time period and culture, but instead he chose to immediately serve the LORD rather than his own comforts. Third, Abraham served speedily. Notice that he "ran from the tent door to meet them", he "hurried into the tent to Sarah", and "ran to the herd" to have a young man prepare it hastily. Remember, this man is 99 years old and he is running around during the "heat of the day"! Fourth, Abraham served generously. The bread Sarah made was from "fine meal" while the meat was "tender and good" after being freshly butchered. He truly gave the best he had to the LORD. Fifth, Abraham served humbly. Notice how he bowed to his guests, called himself a servant, and stood nearby like a waiter available for anything they needed. Sixth, Abraham served cooperatively. He worked with efficient communication to his wife and his servants to serve his guests with both speed and the highest quality work possible. What an example for us to serve personally, immediately, speedily, generously, humbly, and cooperatively!

In Genesis 18:9 – 15, we see Abraham ministering to his family in a more subtle way. Notice how his servants respected him enough to fight alongside in war (Gen. 14), receive circumcision (Gen. 17), and quickly prepare this extravagant meal for strangers. Notice how his wife Sarah eventually repented from her lack of trust in God and this is likely due to the influence of her God-fearing husband. Husbands, remember this: the husband who ministers to the LORD first will naturally find himself ministering to his wife next and the rest of his family.

In Genesis 18:9 – 16, we see Abraham now ministering to a lost world. When God revealed His plan for Sodom and Gomorrah, it was for this very purpose; that Abraham would pray on behalf of these wicked people just like He prays on the behalf of us (Jn 17; Rom. 8:34; Heb. 7:25). Everything that God does in your life as a Christian is to make you more Christ-like. Absolutely everything.

All ministry must be to the LORD first, for if we fail to be a blessing to the LORD, then we will never truly be a blessing to anyone else. Your relationship with God will immediately determine your relationship with everyone else.

FRIEND OF THE WORLD

Genesis 19 records the sad consequences of Lot's gradual spiritual decline. Lot first looked toward Sodom (Gen. 13:10), then pitched his tent near Sodom (Gen. 13:12), and was finally living in Sodom (Gen. 19). However, Sodom was living in Lot long before Lot was living in Sodom. Abraham was a friend of God while Lot was a friend of the world (Jam. 4:4) which resulted in two very different lifestyles and legacies.

At the end of Genesis 19 we see a tragic event where Lot and his two virgin daughters are stranded in a cave, in the mountains, while their former hometown, Sodom, lay completely in ruin. Then, it gets worse. Out of despair, the daughters get their dad so drunk that he'll sleep with them in hopes of bearing children. My friend, this is not the victorious Christian life.

Lot's firstborn bore a son named Moab who would be the forefather of the Moabites. It was the Moabite women who would later seduce Israel to commit sexual immorality and idolatry (Num. 25:1 – 3). Lot's second-born bore a son named Ben-Ammi who would be the forefather of the Ammonites. It was the Ammonites who taught Israel the worship of Molech and the sacrificing of children (1st. Kngs. 11:33; Jer. 32:35). I'm sure Lot had no idea how bad the consequences of his would be. I'm sure when we sin we don't often think of the consequences either.

As dark as this situation may be, there is still hope in this story. There will be a young woman from Moab who meets a man from Judah, marries him, but he dies. She will go back to the land of

Israel with her mother-in-law Naomi and decide to be a worshipper of the one true living God. She will meet a man from Bethlehem named Boaz; her name is Ruth, and she is from Moab. Boaz will marry Ruth, and they will have a son named Obed, who has a son named Jesse, and who is Jesse's son? David. Who comes from the line of David? Jesus Christ the Lord. Truly God works out everything for the good (Rom. 8:28). If you think you've messed up your life so bad that nothing good can come out of it, think again. If God can work through the mess of Lot's life, through the mess of my life, then I have confidence that God can work through the mess of your life and turn something good out of it.

SIN REPEATED

In Genesis 20, we learn three things from Abraham, the trouble-maker: 1) Believers do sin, 2) When believers sin, they suffer, and 3) Sinning believers can be forgiven and restored.

This is the same half-truth, full-lie, that he told Pharaoh back in Egypt 25 years earlier (Gen. 12)! Obviously, wisdom does not come with age. Now, we can't be too hard on Abraham for committing the same sin he did 25 years earlier; some of us commit the same sin every 25 minutes. Remember to examine yourself first and repent before rebuking someone else dealing with the same issue (Matt. 7:3 – 5).

Learn from Abraham's mistake lest you experience Proverbs 26:11 like he did, "As a dog returns to its vomit, so fools repeat their folly."

LET'S PRAY, *"Dear God, thank You for wanting to be my friend. Thank You for giving me examples in the Bible, in history, and in my life, what being Your friend looks like. Please help me to serve You personally, immediately, speedily, generously, humbly, and cooperatively just like*

Abraham did. As I minister to You, help me to better minister to my family and those lost in the world. I look forward to how You will use me today and every day You give me. I ask this in the name of Jesus. Amen."

ACTION POINT

As we discussed earlier, friendship involves service, but it also involves communication. Your Action Point today is simple:

1) Communicate with God by praying throughout the day. Invite Him into every detail of today whether you're eating a meal, running errands, at work, etc. Be His friend by not only talking to Him, but by listening.

2) Communicate with your family by making an effort to go deeper than small talk. Ask about the details of their day, ask about how their relationship with God has been, share stories, laugh together, and if necessary, cry together.

3) Communicate with the lost world today by making a new friend who is not a Christian. Connect with them on something that you both like; for example, music, sports, hobbies, work, etc. Get to know their name, exchange contact info, and maintain consistent communication with them for the purpose of them getting saved and ultimately walking with Jesus with you.

IF YOU'RE WILLING, I trust God is going to use you in a beautiful way today. Now go be a friend of God, your family, and the lost!

DAY TWELVE

GENESIS 21:1 - 22:19

"God didn't ask Abraham to go through with the sacrifice. But one dark Friday, God would provide. The beloved Son of the Father would walk willingly up that hill, carrying the wood on his back. And there he would be slain to save and bless the world." - Glen Scrivener, Evangelist & Author

ISAAC

Isaac, whose name means laughter, is born, and his birth meant four things:

1. The fulfillment of God's promise (Genesis 15:3)
2. The rewarding of patience because Abraham and Sarah had to wait 25 years (James 1:2 - 4).
3. The revelation of God's power because both Abraham and Sarah were way past child-bearing years (Hebrews 11:12).
4. The accomplishing of God's purpose because it was

through Isaac's line that the Messiah would be born (Matthew 1:2).

THERE ARE ALSO five ways that Isaac represents the Christian:

1. Isaac was the second born - When a person receives Christ, they experience the miraculous 2nd birth by the regeneration of the Holy Spirit. God often rejected the firstborn and accepted the second born; not that he predestined them to do so, but God used their actions to prove the spiritual truth of the 2nd birth: Abel was accepted over Cain, Isaac was accepted over Ishmael, Jacob was chosen over Esau, and Ephraim was chosen instead of Manasseh. As a Christian, your 2nd birth of the Spirit is accepted by God as opposed to your 1st birth of the flesh.
2. The joy that he brought - The Luke 15 parables of Jesus are used to illustrate the joy that God has when one sinner comes to repentance: The shepherd rejoiced when he found his lost sheep, the woman rejoiced when she found the lost coin, and the father rejoiced when the prodigal son came home.
3. He grew and was weaned - To be reborn is not the end, but the beginning, and the believer must be continually fed the nutrition of Scripture to be spiritually strong (Matt. 4:4; Heb. 5:12 – 14; 2nd Pet. 3:18). As we mature in the Lord, we must put away childish things (1st Cor. 13:9 – 11) and allow God to "wean us" from the unimportant things of this world that slow us down from becoming stronger men and women of God.
4. Experienced persecution - It was prophesied that Ishmael would be a wild man, a fighter, and that began

with him scoffing at his younger brother Isaac. 2nd Timothy 3:12 – "Yes, and all who desire to live godly will suffer persecution." As a follower of Jesus, that is just the way it is, you will suffer for simply being a Christian.

5. Isaac was born free - Ishmael was born to a slave woman while Isaac was born to a free woman; in the same way, we are first born under the bondage of sin, but then set free because of Jesus Christ in our 2nd birth (Gal. 2:19 – 20).

A SUPERNATURAL CHARACTERISTIC within the Bible is God's way of utilizing real people and real events in the past to prophesy something greater in the future. For example, there are 13 similarities between Isaac and Jesus, none of which are a coincidence. Let me show you:

1. Isaac is the promised seed (Genesis 17:16). Jesus is the promised seed (Galatians 3:16).
2. Isaac's birth was a miracle—it was physically impossible for him to be conceived (Genesis 17:17-19). Jesus' birth was a miracle, being conceived by the Holy Spirit and born of a virgin (Matthew 1:18-25).
3. Abraham loved his only begotten son just as God the Father loves His only begotten Son.
4. Abraham is instructed to sacrifice his son (Genesis 22:1-2). God spared not His only Son (John 3:16, Romans 8:32).
5. Isaac carried the wood on his back that he would be sacrificed on just as Jesus carried the wood of the cross to be crucified.

6. Isaac to be sacrificed on Mount Moriah (Genesis 22:1-2). Jesus was sacrificed on Mount Moriah (Calvary).

7. Isaac was obedient to his father unto death (Genesis 22:5-12). Jesus was obedient to the Father unto death (Philippians 2:5-8).

8. A ram is substituted for Isaac (Genesis 22:13). Christ's death was a substitution for us (2 Corinthians 5:21).

9. Isaac was as good as dead for 3 days, but then brought back alive (Genesis 22:4) just as Jesus was in the tomb for 3 days and then resurrected (Luke 24:6).

10. Abraham sends his oldest servant to select a bride for his son (Genesis 24). The bride responds to the servant even though she is in a foreign country. The Holy Spirit is sent out into the world to seek out the Church. The Church responds even though she is apart from Jesus, but will be known as the Bride of Christ (Ephesians 5:22-33; 6:12).

11. Rebekah, before marrying Isaac, acquires silver and gold (Genesis 24:53). Before the marriage to Christ the bridegroom, the Church acquires gold, silver, and precious stones (1 Corinthians 3:12-15).

12. Isaac went out and brought Rebekah into his mother's tent (Genesis 24:63-67). Jesus meets the Church in the air (1 Thessalonians 4:13-18) and takes her to His Father's house (John 14:1-3).

13. Abraham gives all things to Isaac his son (Genesis 25:5). God has given all things to Jesus, His Son (Ephesians 1:22; Hebrews 1:2).

NAMES OF GOD IN THE OLD TESTAMENT

After an incredibly exhausting 3 days, and the greatest test Abraham has ever experienced, God reveals Himself in a new way, as the LORD who provides. At this point, you might find it interesting the different ways that God reveals Himself in the Old Testament. He is the same today, yesterday, and forevermore, which means that He wants you to experience Him in these ways still. Here are the names of God in the Old Testament:

- YAHWEH-JIREH: "The Lord Will Provide" (Genesis 22:14) – the name memorialized by Abraham when God provided the ram to be sacrificed in place of Isaac.
- YAHWEH-RAPHA: "The Lord Who Heals" (Exodus 15:26) – "I am Yahweh who heals you" both in body and soul. In body, by preserving from and curing diseases, and in soul, by forgiving sin.
- YAHWEH-NISSI: "The Lord Our Banner" (Exodus 17:15), where banner is understood to be a rallying place. This name commemorates the desert victory over the Amalekites.
- YAHWEH-M'KADDESH: "The Lord Who Sanctifies, Makes Holy" (Leviticus 20:8; Ezekiel 37:28) – God makes it clear that He alone, not the law, can cleanse His people and make them holy.
- YAHWEH-SHALOM: "The Lord Our Peace" (Judges 6:24) – the name given by Gideon to the altar he built after the Angel of the Lord assured him he would not die as he thought he would after seeing Him.
- YAHWEH-ELOHIM: "LORD God" (Genesis 2:4; Psalm 59:5) – a combination of God's unique name YHWH and the generic "Lord," signifying that He is the Lord of Lords.
- YAHWEH-TSIDKENU: "The Lord Our Righteousness" (Jeremiah 33:16) – As with Yahweh-M'Kaddesh, it is God alone who provides righteousness to man, ultimately in the person of His Son, Jesus Christ, who became sin for us "that we might become the Righteousness of God in Him" (2 Corinthians 5:21).

- YAHWEH-ROHI: "The Lord Our Shepherd" (Psalm 23:1) – After David pondered his relationship as a shepherd to his sheep, he realized that was exactly the relationship God had with him, and so he declares, "Yahweh is my Shepherd. I shall not want" (Psalm 23:1).
- YAHWEH-SHAMMAH: "The Lord Is There" (Ezekiel 48:35) – the name ascribed to Jerusalem and the Temple there, indicating that the once-departed glory of the Lord (Ezekiel 8—11) had returned (Ezekiel 44:1-4).
- YAHWEH-SABAOTH: "The Lord of Hosts" (Isaiah 1:24; Psalm 46:7) – Hosts means "hordes," both of angels and of men. He is Lord of the host of heaven and of the inhabitants of the earth, of Jews and Gentiles, of rich and poor, master and slave. The name is expressive of the majesty, power, and authority of God and shows that He is able to accomplish what He determines to do.

Here is something important to ponder, that the closer and longer we walk with the LORD, the more He reveals Himself to us.

LET'S PRAY, *"Dear God, thank You that Your word is simple enough for a child to understand and complex enough that scholars have studied it deeply for centuries. Thank You for revealing Yourself to me. I ask that You would help me to see You and experience You for who You really are. Thank You for sacrificing Jesus in my place. You died for me, so help me to live for You. I ask this in the name of Jesus. Amen."*

～

ACTION POINT

In today's reading we learn some very key Christian lessons: 1) Where God guides, God provides. 2) Expect tests from God. 3) Focus on the command, not the explanation. Your Action Point for today, in light of today's reading, is this: Ask yourself the question, "Am I willing to sacrifice everything for Christ?"

GOD MAY NOT ASK you to sell all of your possessions and He may not ask you to move to a 3rd world country for completely selfless mission's work, but what if He did? Are you willing to sacrifice everything for the proclamation of the Gospel and the advancement of His Kingdom? Today, ask God to help you surrender your life, your family, your possessions, and your goals to Him.

THE WORLD IS YET to see what a man or woman can do who is completely surrendered to the Lord Jesus Christ.

DAY THIRTEEN

GENESIS 22:20 - 24:67

"We were promised sufferings. They were part of the program. We were even told, 'Blessed are they that mourn,' and I accepted it. I've got nothing that I hadn't bargained for. Of course it is different when the thing happens to oneself, not to others, and in reality, not imagination." - C.S. Lewis, Author & Theologian (1898 - 1963)

IT HAS LONG BEEN ACCEPTED that the death of your spouse is one of, if not, the most traumatic event a person can experience. As we have just read, Abraham is now facing his new reality and transition of life with the passing of his wife Sarah. C.S. Lewis, in light of his quote above, felt death's disastrous sting at the passing of his wife Joy in 1960. There are many I can think of, and I'm sure you can too, who have been devastated by this unimaginably painful reality; the death of your spouse.

. . .

AT THE END of today's reading I pray that our compassion for widows and the elderly is deepened for the glory of God.

DEATH OF SARAH, GRIEF OF ABRAHAM

Sarah had her own flaws, like we all do, but she still played a key role in God's plan of redemption. As we see her life come to a close there are five important things to notice about Sarah:

1. She is the only woman in the Bible whose age is recorded at death, 127 years (Genesis 23:1)
2. God called her a princess (Genesis 17:15).
3. She is listed in the Hall of Faith (Hebrews 11:11).
4. She is named as a good example for godly women to follow (Isaiah 51:2; 1st Peter 3:1 – 6).
5. Paul used her to show the grace of God in the life of a believer (Galatians 4:21 – 31)

WITH THE PASSING OF SARAH, we see Abraham's tears in Genesis 23:1 – 2. Now, concerning the process of grieving, to cry is not bad. In fact, it is part of God's healing process for a broken heart. Remember, even Jesus wept (John 11:35). There are only two types of people and only two ways to grieve.

For the Christian who has passed away, we cry with hope. Paul says in 1st Thessalonians 4:13, "But I don't want you to be ignorant brethren, concerning those who have fallen asleep, lest you sorrow as others who have no hope." When the Christian passes from this life into the glory and presence of God in Heaven, we ought to rejoice that they are forever healed and experiencing life more abundantly than they ever could have on Earth.

For the non-Christian, we cry with a deep heart-wrenching

sorrow. Psalm 119:136 says, "Rivers of water run down from my eyes because men do not keep Your law." When the unrepentant sinner dies, there is no longer hope for them because they go straight to judgment before God (Hebrews 9:27), to Hell (Matthew 13:50), and then resurrected at the Great White Throne Judgment in the future, but only to the 2nd Death which is to suffer God's wrath forever in the Lake of Fire (Revelation 20:11 – 15).

If you're married, or desiring to be married, I want to encourage you with this: there are no perfect marriages (Yes, this is an encouragement!). Think of the most Christian, godly, couple you know. Have them in your mind? Yes! Even they have problems.

Why do I say this? Abraham and Sarah had problems in their marriage (Obviously!). Yet, God still used them powerfully. Yes, both the husband and wife should daily strive to represent Christ and His Church properly, but don't condemn yourself and with-draw from your spouse when you mess up (Because you will!). Regardless of how your marriage started and even regardless of where you're at right now in your marriage, make it your daily prayer and goal to always improve it for the glory of God.

MARRIAGE OF ISAAC AND REBEKAH

Speaking of marriage, notice how 31 verses are devoted to the creation account while 67 verses are devoted to how Rebekah became Isaac's wife. The answer to "why" is that this event is deeper than history and touches on some important theology. This foreshadows the "mystery" (Eph. 5:32) of marriage representing Christ and the Church. There is a great book I would like to recommend regarding this topic written by a friend of mine named Jay McCarl called The Best Day of Forever.

. . .

Now, in our reading today we see that there are four elements involved in the marriage of Isaac and Rebekah that are also involved in the marriage of Christ and His Church:

1. The will of the father (Vs.1 - 9)
2. The willingness of the servant (Vs.10 - 49)
3. The willingness of the bride (Vs.50 - 60)
4. The welcome of the bridegroom (Vs.61 - 67)

It was the will of Abraham that Isaac receive a bride from his family in the same way God the Father is calling a Bride, a people who are born-again into the family of God, out of the world to be wedded to His Son. It was the willingness of the servant (Likely Eliezer whose name means comforter) to go and bring Isaac's wife in the same way the Spirit of God, sent from the Father, is in the world as a willing Servant gathering a Bride for Jesus (Eph. 1:13 - 14). It was the willingness of the bride, Rebekah, that caused her to be married in the same way that we have a choice to willingly accept or reject Jesus as our Bridegroom (Rom. 10:9, 13). Finally, it was the welcome of the bridegroom Isaac that made their marriage a reality in the same way that one day, the Bride of Christ, will be joined together forever with our Bridegroom Jesus at the marriage supper of the Lamb as recorded in Revelation 19:6 - 9.

If we look closer we see three parallels between the servant and the Holy Spirit:

1. The servant did not speak about himself, but about the one whom he was getting a bride for. (Jn. 15:26; 16:5 – 15)
2. The servant gave gifts as a "down-payment" showing his master's ability & intention just as God the Father has

sealed us by the Holy Spirit to one day be brought to Jesus. (Eph. 1:13 – 14)

3. The servant is not forcing Rebekah to marry Isaac, but merely representing him while giving the facts. (Jn. 16:5 – 15)

There are also six parallels between Rebekah and the Church:

1. Chosen for marriage before they knew it (Eph. 1:3-4).
2. Necessary for the accomplishment of God's eternal purpose (Eph. 3:10-11).
3. Destined to share in the glory of the Son (Jn. 17:22-23).
4. Learn of the Son through his representative. (Jn. 14:26)
5. Must leave all with joy to be with the Son. (Lk. 9:62)
6. Are loved and cared for by the Son. (Eph. 1:3)

THE BIBLE IS TRULY an amazing gift of God to the world. As we have just seen, He orchestrates these real events in history and then uses those same events to foreshadow even greater events that would take place in the future. The Bible is certainly God's love-letter to His creation.

LET'S PRAY, "Dear God, thank You for being the God of all comfort to those in need, and especially those who mourn the loss of a loved one. Thank You for calling me out of the world to not only be a part of Your family, but to also invite others into a relationship with You. Please use me to not only minister to widows, widowers, and the elderly, but to also influence others to do the same. Glorify Yourself through me. I ask this in the name of Jesus. Amen."

∼

ACTION POINT

Today we saw a very important event in the life of Abraham in his old age; the passing of his wife Sarah. We know God's word calls us to care for widows and widowers (James 1:27) as well as the elderly (1st Timothy 5:4 - 8), so today's Action Point is in regards to that.

With regard to widows and widowers: Talk to your local church about what they are already doing to serve those people. Talk about possibly starting a Grief Group to minister to those in the church and in the community who have lost a loved one.

With regard to the elderly: Invite some other Christians to go with you to a local convalescent home and serve them. Some ideas are: 1) Starting a conversation and simply listening to them, 2) Play games with them, and 3) Sing worship songs and read the Bible to them.

WHEN I SERVED at our local convalescent home leading weekly services for about 18 months I remember the sweet times of God using our team to talk, give messages out of the Bible, sing worship songs, bring food, pray with, and serve these people who are often forgotten and alone. Take a step of faith in this way and I guarantee you will be blessed.

DAY FOURTEEN

GENESIS 25:1 - 26:35

"The happiest and holiest children in the world are the children whose fathers succeed in winning both their tender affection and their reverential and loving fear. And they are the children who will come to understand most easily the mystery of the fatherhood of God." - John Piper, Pastor & Author

As a father I must remind myself that God never called me to have godly children, instead, He called me to be a godly parent. Like Abraham, we all make mistakes; sometimes big ones and sometimes small ones, but God, in His grace, can still work all things together for the good (Rom. 8:28). In today's reading we see that Isaac will follow in the footsteps of his dad Abraham to walk with the Lord. Will Isaac himself make mistakes? Absolutely. Will God still work through Isaac's life? Absolutely. The same is true for you.

ABRAHAM AND KETURAH

As Moses begins to close his account of Abraham's life, we see that Abraham "again took a wife", Keturah, and had children with her. 1st Chronicles 1:32 refers to Keturah as his concubine and Vs. 6 seems to confirm this; thus, she was his secondary wife. There is debate as to when this actually happened in Abraham's life. Some say that this is back when he had concubines before he married Sarah, but this is impossible because Vs. 6 says that he gave gifts to the sons of his concubines (plural) and sent them Eastward away from Isaac; thus, Isaac was already alive when this happened. Some hold the view this was before Sarah because, think about it, how can a man over 130 years old still have kids? Either way, this is what the Bible records and its record is true.

ABRAHAM BREATHED HIS LAST

Abraham dies as one of history's most important figures. He is mentioned 70x in the New Testament and is only exceeded by two people; Moses, who is mentioned 80x in the New Testament and Jesus who is mentioned over 900x.

We get a quick synopsis as to what happened to Abraham's many other children and we see that Abraham is transitioning his wealth, power, servants, and ultimately the Covenant to his promised son, Isaac.

It's important to mention that Abraham did not see the promise of God fulfilled in his lifetime, but he trusted that God would be faithful. I encourage you to read Hebrews 11:8 - 10 regarding Abraham's life and mindset. Keep this truth in mind as you continue to grow and serve Christ advancing His kingdom; you may not see the fruit of your labor right away. No matter what role you play in a person's life or in a situation, there are those who pioneer, those who continue the work, and those who reap the fruits of that hard work, but no matter what, God is working through them all for His glory (1st Corinthians 3:6 - 9). Faithfulness is more important that the results of your faithfulness.

FAMILIES OF ISHMAEL AND ISAAC

Genesis 25:12 – 28 serves as another transitionary passage. Moses records the families of Ishmael and his death to then transition into Isaac's family because that is the lineage of the Messiah, Jesus. Notice how God was faithful to His promise back in Genesis 17:20 regarding the 12 princes who would then become 12 Arab nations from Ishmael. Now, with the death of Ishmael, Isaac will take center stage as the Plan of Redemption continues to unfold.

What God says in Genesis 25:23 is uncultural because it was always the firstborn who was to be the leader or dominant one; however, He says, "the older shall serve the younger". Esau (Whose name means "hairy" or "rough") is the beginning of the nation of Edom while Jacob (Whose name means "heel-catcher" or "deceiver") is the beginning of the nation of Israel. As these two nations grew, Edom was not only a contention in Israel's life, but they were eventually subdued by the nation of Israel (1st Samuel. 14:47-48; 2nd Samuel. 8:13-14). The messages of Obadiah and Malachi were largely against Edom and described their future destruction.

ESAU SELLS HIS BIRTHRIGHT

Jacob knew that the birthright was valuable and he wanted it. Passages like Deuteronomy 21:17 and 1 Chronicles 5:1-2 tell us the birthright involved both a material and a spiritual dynamic. The son of the birthright received a double portion than anyone else of the inheritance, and he also became the head of the family and the spiritual leader upon the passing of the father. In the case of this family, the birthright determined who would inherit the covenant God made with Abraham regarding the land, the nation, and the Messiah.

So, if the birthright was so important, why does Genesis 25:34 say that Esau "despised his birthright"? Esau's character as a fornicator and profane person (Hebrews 12:16) shows God was entirely correct in choosing Jacob over Esau to carry on the birthright, even though Jacob was younger. Though Esau's character was not the basis for God's choosing, because God chose before they were born, Esau's character showed the ultimate wisdom of God's choice.

Here's something important for us as Christian's to know; we have a spiritual birthright as children of God. Ephesians 1:3 – 14 shows us a treasury of riches that is in our birthright; every spiritual blessing, the blessing of being chosen in Jesus, adoption into God's family, total acceptance by God in Christ, redemption from our slavery to sin, true and total forgiveness, the riches of God's grace, the revelation and knowledge of the mystery of God's will, an eternal inheritance, the guarantee of the indwelling Holy Spirit right now. We too, as God's children, can despise our birthright by not walking in obedience to Him though we have received so much from Him. May we cherish our spiritual birthright and not despise it.

ISAAC, ABIMELECH, AND THE PHILISTINES

Genesis 26 records a glimpse of Isaac's life where we see him follow in the footsteps of his father Abraham in both his failure and success. Like father, like son, Isaac falls for the same sins as his father Abraham when he was tempted to run during a famine (Vs.1 – 6) and tempted to lie regarding his wife (Vs.7 – 11). However, we also see Isaac victoriously following in his dad's footsteps towards the end of the chapter. The Philistines had stopped up the wells which Abraham had dug to show Isaac that he was not welcome there; thus, Isaac and his servants had to clean out the wells. The strife between Isaac and the Philistines continued at Esek (*contention*), then to Sitnah (*enmity*), then finally Isaac moved away from the Philistines where he dug a well and called it Rehoboth (*roominess*).

It is at Beersheba where God comforts, encourages, and reassures Isaac in the midst of his trouble. Isaac then builds an altar to worship, a tent to temporarily dwell, and digs a well to be refreshed. Just as Isaac took after his father Abraham as a worshiper, pilgrim, and well digger, so we should also be worshipers, pilgrims, and dig deep into the spiritual well that we may partake of the water of God's written word (Eph. 5:26).

LET'S PRAY, "*Dear God, thank You for the gift of another day. Thank You for the time I get to spend in Your word, seeing You work in the events of history, and showing me how it applies to my life now. Thank You for using Abraham and Isaac for Your glory even though they made mistakes; thank You for wanting to use me even though I make mistakes. Help me to be teachable, moldable, and always willing to be corrected. As You are leading me and using others to disciple me, please use me to effectively disciple other people. Help me to lead by example in what it means to follow Jesus in all areas of life. I ask this in the name of Jesus. Amen.*"

∾

ACTION POINT

Today we saw the importance of Godly Parenting with regard to Abraham and Isaac. With that being said, your Action Point today is, 1) If you're a parent, start implementing these 10 tips and 2) If you're not a parent, then start implementing these 10 tips with your spiritual kids; those whom you are discipling. Here are 10 Tips for Godly Parenting:

1. Teach them early and often about the Gospel.
2. Teach them that their identity is in God and His word; not their performance or the opinions of others.
3. Study your child; learn their personality, likes, dislikes, desires, and talents so you can connect with them in specific ways.
4. Budget time in each day to teach Biblical truth. Remember to make it fun!
5. Set clear boundaries and discipline consistently as needed. You're in charge, not the child.
6. Give opportunities to learn, work, grow, and have new healthy experiences.
7. Don't always hide your mistakes; instead, use them as opportunities for your child to learn from.
8. Encourage and work with your child to set goals for the short-term and long-term, then, guide them to achieving these goals.
9. Balance work and play. Teach and show that a God-honoring life can be fun and exciting!
10. In everything you do, always reinforce that our greatest goal, every day, is to glorify God.

DAY FIFTEEN

GENESIS 27:1 - 28:5

"What was there to like about Jacob? He was an opportunist, co-conspirator, shifty, untrustworthy, negligent, and a father who picked favorites. Yet God said, '*Jacob I loved, but Esau I hated*' (Romans 9:13). God blessed him with many children, a productive lifestyle, and a long life. Jacob's story reminds believers that God is in the business of transforming our struggles for His purposes and our good." - Crystal McDowell, Contributor to whatchristianswanttoknow.com

~

JACOB'S DECEPTION AND ISAAC'S BLESSING

If Christianity were a man-made ideology for others to follow, it would not have included Genesis 27 or other embarrassing passages of prominent figures in the Bible. It's important to note that the good, bad, and the ugly were included in Scripture to demonstrate at least two things: 1) The reliability of the Bible by its authenticity, and 2) God can use messed up people like you and me.

Now, before we can talk about Jacob's deception, we need to discuss his father. Martin Luther calculates Isaac's age here at 137, which is widely accepted; however, we'll see he lives for another 43 years. Here's how Isaac's character did not help the situation. First of all, we see that Isaac is putting himself before the Lord at the end of his life. When Abraham prepared for death, his concern was for his son to get a bride and maintain the covenant promise. When King David came to his end, he made arrangements for God's temple to be built. When Paul was facing his execution, he instructed Timothy to be faithful just as he was faithful. When Isaac was about to die, all he wanted was one last meal. Secondly, he was disobeying God's command. Before the boys were born God had already prophesied that the older would serve the younger; yet, Isaac still wanted to give the blessing to Esau. Thirdly, Isaac lived by his feelings. In light of Isaac's spiritual heritage, you would think that at this time he would be calling on the name of the Lord; instead, he was depending upon his own senses of taste, touch, hearing, and smelling. He began to live by the natural instead of the supernatural. Of course, Rebekah, Jacob, and Esau are all walking in the flesh here too, but Isaac is the father and supposed to be the spiritual leader.

Jacob lies about six things here: 1) His name (Vs.19), 2) obeying his father's wishes (Vs.19), 3) the food being from him (Vs.19), 4) the LORD aiding him (Vs.20), 5) his identity (Vs.21 - 24), and 6) his love (Vs.27). The kiss Jacob gave his father was hypocritical and not loving, for if he truly loved his father he would have been honest with him. If you want to truly show your love to God and people then be honest with God and people.

It's also important to note that Rebekah and Jacob's deception were unnecessary because God had already promised the blessing to Jacob. If they simply listened and obeyed God then they would have bypassed the bitterness, hate, and division that would soon follow.

ESAU'S ANGER

Why did Esau react the way that he did? It was because he wanted the material blessing rather than the spiritual; he didn't care about his birthright or being a part of God's covenant originally given to his grandfather Abraham. Genesis 25:34 records that he despised his birthright while Hebrews 12:16 reveals that Esau was a fornicator, profane, and sold his birthright for a morsel of food. Esau was so consumed with anger that he planned to kill his brother after their father Isaac died and the days of mourning ended. When Rebekah heard of this, she told Jacob to go to her brother Laban's home in Haran. She feared not only that Jacob would be killed, but that Esau in his pursuits might be killed. To explain Jacob's departure, she told Isaac that she was afraid to have Jacob marry a Hittite woman as Esau had done; thus, she was sending him away. Little did she know that he would not return for over 20 years, and when he would, she would have already died. Remember, the Savior of the world is coming from one dysfunctional family after another.

Let's briefly look at some important things regarding Isaac in this passage. In Genesis 27:33 it says that, "… Isaac trembled exceedingly…" A Hebrew literal translation would be, "Isaac trembled most excessively with a great trembling." Why did Isaac react like this when he realized that he blessed Jacob? Because now he finally woke from his spiritual slumber. He remembered what God said (Gen. 25:23) and that he was going against God's will trying to bless Esau. Notice also what Isaac says to Esau in Genesis 27:39 – 40. This predicts that the Edomites would live in fertile lands, be warriors, be subject to the Israelites, and would one day rebel against them. This prophecy of Isaac upon his son Esau was fulfilled in the reign of Joram, king of Judah (2nd Kings 8:20 – 22).

COVENANT TRANSFERRED TO JACOB

Padan Aram was situated in Northern Mesopotamia and located in the same area was Haran where remnants of Abraham's family resided. Isaac readily agreed to have Jacob find a wife in Haran and was most likely remembering his own experiences when his dad Abraham commanded the servant to find his wife, Rebekah.

The covenant blessings were originally given to Abraham (Gen. 12:1 – 3), then to Isaac (Gen. 17:19), and now to Jacob. Jacob is by no means worthy of this; the only reason he is inheriting such a blessing is because of God's infinite wisdom and grace. I'm grateful that God continues bless us despite our own mistakes. My friend, don't be discouraged and think your failures cause you to be unusable by God. You and I are in the lineage of a long line of sinning saints that God still used for His glory. We're in good company.

LET'S PRAY, *"Dear God, thank You for being the God of so many chances. Thank You for examples in the Bible like Jacob, and others, who remind me that I don't need to be perfect to be used by You, I simply need to be willing. Please help me to never fall for the enemy's condemnation, but to always submit to Your conviction. Please use me to encourage people that their past does not need to dictate their future. I ask this in the name of Jesus. Amen."*

∾

ACTION POINT

Today we talked about Jacob, an example of someone who, though made mistakes, was still blessed and used by God. Your Action Point today is two-fold:

1) If you know someone that feels their sin causes them to be

unusable by God, then make an effort today to encourage them via text, phone-call, in-person, etc. that if they confess their sins to God, He is faithful to cleanse them (1st Jn. 1:9) and use them for His purposes. Ask the Lord to guide your conversation.

2) Take a moment to pray for those who feel that their sinful pasts cause them to be unusable by God. Pray for freedom. Ask God to help them walk as a new creation in Christ and that they don't need to look back.

DAY SIXTEEN

GENESIS 28:6 - 29:30

"Pray as though everything depended on God. Work as though everything depended on you." - Augustine of Hippo, Theologian & Author (354 - 430)

ESAU

Isaac called Jacob, blessed him, and sent him to Padan Aram, a district in Mesopotamia, so that he would find a wife among his mother's people instead of the Canaanites. This inspired Esau to try and regain his father's blessing by marrying a daughter of Ishmael, thinking that would please him.

Many Christians do what Esau did; doing whatever it is that they *think* will please God. Proverbs 14:12 says, "There is a way that seems right to a man, but its end is the way of death." One of the many important reasons to consistently read and study God's word is not only to know Him, but to know what pleases Him.

JACOB'S JOURNEY, DREAM, AND VOW

Jacob, who according to Scripture was more of a home-body, now begins a 500 mile journey from Beersheba to Haran. It was a 3 day journey from Beersheba to Bethel and I'm sure many questions filled his mind such as, "Is Esau going to follow and kill me? Am I going to have enough food, water, and shelter? What is my future going to look like?"

As Jacob spent his first night at Bethel he had a dream which was really a prophecy regarding the coming Messiah; Jesus who was the ladder to come, the only way to Heaven and eternal life. Jesus says in John 1:51, "Most assuredly, I say to you, hereafter you shall see heaven open, and the angels of God ascending and descending upon the Son of Man."

At Bethel we see a pivotal moment in Jacob's life where he has the 1st of 5 appearances that God would make to him as recorded in Scripture. The same God that cared for his grandfather Abraham, his father Isaac, is now caring for him. Take a moment to reread the promises that God gives to Jacob in Genesis 28:13 – 15. This is an Old Testament example of a New Testament truth. Philippians 1:6 says, "... being confident of this very thing, that He who began a good work in you will complete it until the day of Jesus Christ..." The fact that you woke up today is evidence that God is still not done with you and there are plans He desires you to fulfill. In the same way God was not done with Jacob, God is not done with you.

Just like Abraham and Isaac, Jacob is now enrolled in the School of Faith and there is much to learn. Jacob was 77 when he left Beersheba and began his 500 mile journey North towards Haran, where he would spend 20 years working for his uncle Laban, 33 years back in Canaan, spend his last 17 years of his life in Egypt, and then buried in the cave of Machpelah in Hebron.

JACOB'S MARRIAGE

Jesus made it clear that not everyone is called to marriage (Matt. 19:1-12), but with Jacob, marriage wasn't an option, it was inevitable. The success of the covenant promises originally given to Abraham were dependent upon Jacob having a wife, building a family that would be called the nation of Israel, and those people bringing about the Jewish Messiah.

Jacob survives his 500 mile journey, arrives to Haran, and starts giving orders to these local shepherds. Now, two reasons have been proposed as to why Jacob started administrating a people he'd never met: 1) He actually knew better and 2) He saw Rachel, it was love at first sight, and he was trying to impress her. He acts as if he has the authority, removes this boulder from the well himself, and proceeds to water her sheep. The kiss he gave Rachel was cultural, a simple kiss on the cheek as a greeting, but it's not clear why he started crying. Some have suggested he was overflowing with tears of joy at the thought of meeting his potential wife. Either way, this must've been awkward for Rachel to experience.

The offer to work 7 years for Rachel to be his bride was essentially a dowry. In this culture at this time, every member of the family worked in the family business; therefore, to lose a family member to marriage was to lose an employee and the work they could've produced. There is nothing in Scripture that would suggest Jacob was lazy, in fact we see that he is quite the hard worker; however, he has never worked as a servant before.

Now, with regard to the dastardly deed Laban committed against Jacob, I can't even imagine how angry and frustrating this situation must've been. Remember, in this culture and time period, the father had absolute authority over the family which is how this deceptive switch was even possible; Laban forced it. Laban got exactly what he wanted; free labor for 14 years and 2 of his daughters married. I'm sure he internally congratulated himself on the success of his scheme. Even through something like this, God is going to work out all things for good... again. Food for thought: You never know just how much of a servant you are until you start getting treated like one.

WORK IS A BLESSING, NOT A CURSE

The key theme I would like us to highlight today is on the topic of work. Work is not a curse (Though you might think so!). In the beginning, when there was no sin, God commanded Adam to work for Him (Gen. 1:28; 2:15). Today, in all aspects of life, God commands us to work for Him (1st Cor. 10:31; Col. 3:23). In Heaven, when all sin has been punished and we enjoy perfection with our Creator, God will still have us work (Rev. 22:3). You see, work has always been a God-given opportunity to please your Maker. Work is to be joyful! Not always because of what we're doing, but Who we're doing it for. This is why it's reprehensible for a Christian to live a lifestyle of laziness. Jacob exemplified hard work, according to the Scriptures, even under horrible circumstances. As God's people, it's time for us to let our light shine by being the hardest worker in any environment and under any circumstance so that people may see our good work and glorify our Father in Heaven (Matt. 5:16).

LET'S PRAY, *"Dear God, please forgive me for the times I've been lazy. I'm sorry for dishonoring You. You deserve my very best and I need Your help to do that. Help me to passionately work for You out of love and worship, not out of obligation or chore. Today, please give me laser-focus on the tasks I have. Help me to accomplish quality work by being detail oriented and help me to produce quantity of work by not wasting precious time. I ask this in the name of Jesus. Amen."*

~

ACTION POINT

Today's Action Point is more about mindset rather than a specific task. Our opening quote today from Augustine was, "Pray as though everything depended on God. Work as though everything depended on you." This phrase has helped keep me both desperate for God while simultaneously working to the best of my God-given abilities.

Jacob clearly worked under horrible conditions and for a down-right deceptive employer; yet, he still worked hard and honestly. Your Action Point for today, and every day, is to pray as if everything depends on God while working as if everything depends on you. Whether you have a bad teacher in school or a bad employer at work, seek to outperform, outwork, and outlast every student and employee. Remember, you're not doing this for people to see how great you are. Instead, you're doing this for people to see your excellent grades, your quality work ethic, and perseverance so they would glorify your Father who is in Heaven (Matt. 5:16) who is your ultimate Boss (Col. 3:23).

"Looking at history, I believe God often uses very tangible factors to spur his people to action. I sense that God has been moving his people in remarkably similar ways—across the United States and beyond—to make our ancient commitment of service to orphans again a defining feature of the church." - Jedd Medefind, President of Christian Alliance for Orphans

CHILDREN OF ISRAEL, BIRTH OF A NATION

At this point, let's get a recap of the 12 sons of Israel, in order of their birth, who would later become the 12 tribes of Israel:

- Reuben (*Behold, a son*), son of Leah
- Simeon (*Hearing*), son of Leah
- Levi (*Joined*), son of Leah
- Judah (*Praise*), son of Leah
- Dan (*Judge*), son of Bilhah
- Naphtali (*Wrestling*), son of Bilhah

- Gad (*A troop or good fortune*), son of Zilpah
- Asher (*Happy*), son of Zilpah
- Issachar (*Hire*), son of Leah
- Zebulun (*Dwelling*), son of Leah
- Joseph (Adding), son of Rachel
- Benjamin (*Son of my right hand*), son of Rachel

As you read this account of the family of Israel, do you see how crooked their priorities are? Where is prayer? Where is worship? Where is unity? Where is the humility to work things out? Ultimately, where is the love towards God and one another? These foundational principles are nowhere to be found because everyone has decided to walk according to the flesh and not according to the Spirit.

Not only were there problems with the adults, but how do you think the kids feel being raised in such a dysfunctional household? The reality of hurting kids who are orphaned, abused, neglected, in foster care, or in toxic households is the main topic of discussion for today.

JACOB AND LABAN: AGREEMENT

Genesis 30:25 – 43 records the beginning of the separation between Jacob and Laban. By the time of this passage, Laban had 14 years of experience that Jacob had been a hard-working, detailed-oriented, and excellent servant; therefore, he wanted him to stick around. Though Jacob has not exemplified much spiritual leadership in the past 14 years, he still knows he needs to go back to the Promised Land and answer God's calling on his life. Jacob, therefore, negotiates a deal with his uncle Laban. They agree that Jacob will take all of the blemished livestock while Laban will take all of the solid. On the surface, this seemed like a good idea to Laban, but little did he know he was being deceived by Jacob who had some effective techniques. Though Jacob's methods were deceptive, God is still going to make him prosperous; not because Jacob is good, but because God is good and He still has a plan Jacob needs to fulfill.

Before we move on, do you see Christ in this? This shepherd is willing to take all of the undesirable to himself as his reward for his suffering. One day, about 1,900 years later, the Good Shepherd would come from Heaven, through the line of Judah, suffer unto death, and now reigns victoriously taking us dirty sinners to be made His sheep whom He made white as snow.

JACOB AND LABAN: SEPARATION

By the time we reach Genesis 31, Jacob has been 500 miles away from the Promised Land for 20 years. He has unfinished business with his father and brother, but before he leaves, we see his escape from and confrontation with Laban.

Before Jacob made his escape, God commanded Jacob to go, but how did He do that? The same way that God often speaks to us. Firstly, God spoke to Jacob through the inner witness of the heart. Six years earlier, God had put the desire into Jacob to return to the Promised Land (Gen. 30:25). Now, not every longing in the human heart is the voice of God, and we must always exercise prayerful discernment, but our Shepherd does speak to His sheep and we can know His voice (Jn. 10:27). Secondly, God spoke through the outward circumstances of life. Toward the end of these final 6 years, Jacob noticed that his in-laws were not as friendly as before due to jealousy. Circumstances aren't always the hand of God pointing out His way, but they can certainly be indicators. Thirdly, God spoke through the truth of His word. This is truly the most important because it is through the unchanging revelation of God's desires through His written word that we can know His general will. When you walk in the general will of God, His specific will for your life often naturally unfolds. As the story of Jacob unfolds you discover that God spoke to him at every important crisis in his life such as leaving home (Gen. 28:12 – 15), returning home (Gen. 31:1 – 13), meeting Esau (Gen. 32:24), visiting Bethel (Gen. 35:1), and moving to Egypt (Gen. 46:1 – 4). As your story unfolds, and you seek the will of God, He will speak to you as well.

On a side note, did you read Genesis 31:36 - 42? Jacob has been holding back that speech for 20 years and I'm sure he rehearsed many times to himself. What a moment to have witnessed such a rebuke!

JACOB AND LABAN: COVENANT

The definition of the word Mizpah is watchtower which was used to name the heap or covenant that was made between Jacob and Laban. Today, the Mizpah benediction is seen as a positive, bonding, and emotional statement that is to say, "May the Lord watch over us while we're apart." However, that's not what Laban meant. What Laban meant was more like, "Because we're not going to see each other anymore, may God watch you to judge and punish you if you mistreat my daughters!" This was not so much a blessing as much as it was a warning.

THE PRIMARY INDIVIDUALS in our passage today are Jacob and Laban, but I want us to focus on some innocent bystanders; Jacob's kids. The reality of innocent children in unhealthy households is what I would like us to consider today. My wife and I have a special place in our heart for at risk youth; kids who aren't given the same opportunities to succeed as some of their peers. Throughout our marriage we have housed numerous people who were in a season of need, fostered kids, and have worked closely with struggling families. This work often involves late nights, long talks, tears, painful heartbreak over situations, and lots of desperate prayer for God to bring healing to hurting households.

As Christ's ambassadors of His kingdom, the Church is called to play their God-given role of defending the defenseless (Ps. 82:3-4; Prov. 31:8-9; Is. 1:17); specifically, children. This is not optional. This is our duty.

LET'S PRAY, *"Dear God, thank You for adopting me into Your family. Thank You for not just saying You care, but demonstrating Your compassion in the life, death, and resurrection of Jesus. Please help me to now be a reflection of Your heart towards hurting kids around me; whether they're in unhealthy households, in foster care, or in need of any kind. Please raise up Your Church to step boldly, compassionately, and wisely into the arena of reaching kids for Your glory. I ask this in the name of Jesus. Amen."*

∼

ACTION POINT

Today's Action Point is in light of Jacob's kids who were no doubt being hurt by the sin of their parents and those around them. I want to share a concept that I find is a great way for the Christian to respond practically to the crisis of kids without families.

Adopt a child. If you can't adopt, then foster. If you can't foster, then sponsor. If you can't sponsor, then volunteer. If you can't volunteer, then donate. If you can't donate, then educate. If you can't educate, then pray. The point is that all of us can do something. Take some time to ask the Lord what He would like you and your family to do. It is our God-given privilege and duty to be an extension of His love.

P.S. - At the time of this writing, our family received guardian-ship over a 17 year old boy who has been with us for almost a year. Please pray for God's perfect will to be accomplished in his life.

DAY EIGHTEEN

GENESIS 32:1 - 33:20

"God will meet you in your anguish, fear, and uncertainty. But he may not meet you in the way you expect or desire. Your greatest ally may show up looking at first like your adversary, inciting you to wrestle with him. If so, remember Jacob. There are multiple blessings in the wrestling. You may not need soft words of comfort, you may not need to be left alone with your thoughts, you may not need sleep, you may not even need a healthy hip! What you need is God's blessing! So when God calls you to wrestle with him in prayer, it is an invitation to receive his blessing. Stay with him and don't give up. Do not let him go until he blesses you! He loves to bless that kind of tenacious faith and you will come out transformed." - Jon Bloom, Staff Writer at DesiringGod.org

JACOB PREPARES TO MEET ESAU

As you study Jacob's actions during this crisis time in his life, you see illustrated the conflicts all of us occasionally experience between faith and fear, trusting God and scheming, asking God for help and then doing what we want anyway. An important lesson we learn is that a crisis doesn't make a man; it shows what a man is made of.

In Genesis 32:9 – 12 we see Jacob's prayer, and though it is one of the great prayers recorded in Scripture, it was prayed by a man whose faith was very weak. He was like the father of the demonized child who cried out, "Lord, I believe; help my unbelief!" (Mk. 9:24).

I want us to notice the 5 reasons Jacob gives to God to deliver him from Esau and each of them have an application for us:

1. God's Covenant (Vs. 9a) - God made a covenant to Abraham which was passed down to Isaac, then Jacob, and it was on that basis by which Jacob approached God. The lesson is that God's people today approach the throne of grace on the basis of the new covenant by Jesus' blood (Heb. 8:6 – 13).

2. God's Command (Vs. 9b) - Jacob knew it was God's command for him to leave Haran and go back to Canaan; yet, he is still in fear that he may not live to get back to Canaan! The lesson is that where God guides, God provides.

3. God's Care (Vs. 10) - Jacob speaks of how God has blessed him tremendously by going alone to Haran with nothing but his staff and then leaving with abundant wealth. The question he asks is, "Why would You do all of this God only to have me murdered by my brother?" The lesson is that as a Christian, God will not take you home to Heaven unless He is finished using you on Earth.

4. God's Purposes (Vs. 11) - Jacob wasn't thinking only of himself, but of his family, and God's plan involving them. Little did Jacob know that the Messiah would

come through his son Judah and that Paul the Apostle, who would come from his son Benjamin, would take the Gospel to the Gentiles. The lesson is that you are also destined for something greater than yourself; to be a part of God's global mission to save the lost.

5. God's Promise (Vs. 12) - Jacob reminded the Lord of the promises He made back in Bethel over 20 years ago. What Jacob is saying is, "If my brother kills me and my family, then Your promise will not come to pass!" The lesson is that what God has said is as good as done; we can trust that His promises and prophesies are a sure foundation.

You would think that after such a prayer, Jacob would be confident that the Lord would protect him, but instead he plots again. Now, we can't be too harsh on Jacob because how often do we act the same way? We can have this beautiful experience with God in prayer, in Sunday service, at a conference, etc. and then, moments later, we walk in the flesh. It's important to disregard our fears and simply do what God has said.

JACOB MEETS GOD

In Genesis 32:22 - 33 we find Jacob completely alone and that is often when God speaks clearest to us; when we're separated from the noise of the world. To Abraham the pilgrim, God met him as a traveler (Gen. 18). To Joshua the general, God came to him as the Commander of the Lord's army (Josh. 5:13-15). As someone who wrestled with his brother, dad, uncle, and even his wives, God came to him as a wrestler. Now, this situation of course, is not an equal match. Think of a UFC world champion play-fighting with his 2 year old son; there is no contest. God could have simply spoken Jacob out of existence if He wanted to. So what do we learn? Those whom God greatly uses, He often greatly breaks.

Before God could continue to use Jacob to carry the covenant promises, He needed to break Jacob of himself. If you honestly want to be greatly used by God, then He needs to first break you of your past life, your carnal desires, and anything else that is displeasing to Him. I encourage you to read Hosea's commentary on this passage in Hosea 12:3 - 4.

JACOB MEETS ESAU

Jacob had not seen Esau in over 20 years, and as he drew near, Jacob lapsed back into fearfulness by bowing himself to the ground seven times (Vs.3) and referring himself as Esau's servant (Vs.5). When Esau suggested that they travel back together, Jacob pretended that this would be impossible because of the slow pace required by the children and the young animals. Jacob promised to meet Esau in Seir (Edom), although he had no intention of doing so due to fear. No doubt Jacob is still unsure if his brother still wants to kill him.

HOWEVER, didn't Jacob just have a literal encounter with God and was blessed by Him? How quick we are to be like Jacob by getting onto a spiritual roller-coaster; one moment we're up, one moment we're down. Sometimes we can go from this intimate moment with God either alone with Him, or in a Sunday service, or at a conference, and then moments later deliberately sin, exemplify a lack of faith, and walk in fear. We need to get off the roller-coaster and simply walk with God.

JACOB SETTLES IN SHECHEM

Seir (Edom) is Southeast of Mahanaim and Jacob goes the opposite direction to Shechem which is Northwest. Instead of returning to Bethel, he settles himself and his family into the wicked city of Shechem. It is because of Jacob's fear-filled and deceitful disobedience that we see the tragic results of Genesis 34.

IT SADDENS my heart to see someone have a beautiful encounter with God and then drift from their Savior over time. You cannot live a healthy Christian life based on an experience with God you had in the past; you need to experience Him every day, every moment. Encounter Him, He's waiting for you.

LET'S PRAY, *"Dear God, please humble me. Please greatly break me so You can greatly use me. Help me to get off the spiritual roller-coaster, and instead, have a consistent walk with You. Help me to be unstoppably intense in my pursuit of You. God I want to know You! As I deepen in my relationship with You, please help me to call others to do the same. I ask this in the name of Jesus. Amen."*

∿

ACTION POINT

Jacob met God before he met Esau. In the same way, we need to meet God before we meet our own Esau; those issues of the day we must face.

Here is your Action Point for the day: Make a Daily Devotional Plan and stick to it.

HERE IS my personal plan that I use when I wake up:

1) Read my Personal Declarations. (It may sound weird, but you can contact me personally for exactly what they are and why I do it)

2) Read through the Bible in a year using a 365 Daily Reading

Plan. When I finish Revelation I start right back in Genesis the next day. (If reading is difficult for you, then use audiobooks!)

3) Spend some time talking to God. This is where making a Prayer List is helpful; a list of people, problems, situations, and even goals that you are praying for. Remember, the most important part of prayer is your praise to Him. Refrain from simply giving God your "grocery list" of needs and walking away. Meet with Him. Love Him. Commune with Him.

I CAN SPEAK from experience that my relationship to God determines my relationship to everyone and everything else. Your alone time with God is the most important part of your day and it determines the rest of your day. Make a plan. Stick to it.

"Assault survivors respond differently. There's no right or wrong way to react after being sexually abused. The assault can be so overwhelming that we may respond in three ways - fight, flee, or freeze." — Dana Arcuri, Author & Speaker

GOD'S COMMAND was that Jacob return to Bethel (31:13) and then to his home where Isaac lived, which was Hebron (35:27). Instead, he stayed in Succoth, and then settled near Shechem (*Modern day Samaria*). The name of the LORD is not mentioned once in this chapter; therefore, we see the consequences of when you don't allow God to lead you, but instead allow you to lead you. It is for that reason that we see carelessness (Gen. 34:1), defilement (Gen. 34:2 - 5), deception (Gen. 34:6 - 24), and vengeance (Gen. 34:25 - 31).

CARELESSNESS

In Vs. 1, we see carelessness on the part of Dinah, but primarily on the part of her father, Jacob. There are many questions that arise from this situation, "Was Dinah naive? Rebellious? Ignorant of the land of the pagans? Why was it important she got to know the other women?" The greatest question though is, "Why did her father Jacob allow this?"

A lesson to parents is that you absolutely need to be involved with your child's life; know their friends, what they're doing on social media, what music and movies are influencing them, how they're doing in school, and most of all, what their relationship with God is like.

A lesson to children, those still under the authority of your parents, there will come a time that you launch into your own life and family, but that time is not now. Obey your parents, listen to the wise counsel of older Christians, and learn from their life experiences so you can mature leaps and bounds ahead of your peers for the glory of God.

Instead of being obedient to lead his family to Bethel, Jacob was disobedient and led his family to Shechem. When we disobey God, we're not only putting ourselves in unnecessary danger, but our entire family as well.

DEFILEMENT

In this chapter we see the word "defilement" used 3x to describe Shechem's horrific offense (Gen. 34:5, 15, 27). Shechem said he loved Dinah (Gen. 34:3), but true love does not rape (Gen. 34:5) and hold someone captive (Gen. 34:26).

Many in this generation are driven intensely by their sexual passions and believe mere physical attraction is love when in reality it is the empty, ultimately unsatisfying, shell of lust. God is the author of love, romance, and sex; therefore, in order to experience the fullness of each we must play the game of life using His manual called the Bible.

Notice Jacob's response to his daughter getting raped (Gen. 34:5). This is the reaction of a cowardly father, an apathetic father, or both. Where is the parental care? Where is the godly leadership? It is nowhere with the dad; therefore, the sons decide to take action because their father won't.

Everyone is a leader because everyone has influence and the best leaders take initiative under critical circumstances. Learn from the mistakes of Jacob and others so you can become the best version of yourself that God intended.

DECEPTION

Genesis 34:9 is a clear indication that Satan is working behind the scenes, influencing the situation, and trying to destroy the covenant line. Just as God is interweaving His plan of redemption throughout the Bible we also see Satan, in his futility, trying to sabotage it.

The reason Hamor and Shechem were so willing to have themselves and the men of their city circumcised is because that would be their "foot in the door" to ultimately absorb all of Israel's wealth (Gen. 34:23). Notice that both sides are deceiving each other! With regard to Jacob's family, as soon as they pushed God out of their life, that's when they started acting just like the world.

As you read through the events of Genesis 34 we are left to wonder, "Where is Jacob in all of this?!" It's a shame when sons need to take action because their father won't. Here's where it gets personal. It's a shame when other people need to bear your responsibilities because you choose not to. From one father to another, I pray we rise up to be the strong spiritual leaders our families need.

VENGEANCE

As the chapter comes to a close we find ourselves in a traumatic tragedy. Not only did these boys commit mass murder, high-scale theft, destruction, and perversion of God's holy sign of the covenant, but most reprehensible of all, they misrepresented God entirely. What do you think the pagan nations around them were thinking as they saw those who claimed to follow the one true God act like this? Certainly, there are no godly men in this chapter. If only Jacob obeyed the Lord by taking his family to Bethel this would have all been avoided. Even Jacob's response is a reflection of his pernicious, selfish, heart.

THOUGH THIS IS a chapter of catastrophe, not all hope is lost. God has not given up on the covenant family. Though it seems darkness has consumed mankind, God's light will inevitably shine and cause freedom once again.

LET'S PRAY, *"Dear God, please forgive me for the times I have disobeyed You. Please restore those relationships I've hurt from my own selfishness. Please break my heart over my sin. Build me up into the person You desire me to be. I pray for all those who have suffered sexual assault of any kind; heal them of their pain, restore them from their trauma, and use them to testify of Your power to work all things for good. Help Your Church to raise awareness of, educate about, defend from, and combat against the sin of sexual assault. I ask this in the name of Jesus. Amen."*

ACTION POINT

This event in Genesis is known as the "Dinah Incident" is one that reminds all of us that sexual assault is a horrific reality in our world. Your Action Point today is to take one or more of the following recommendations for you and your church to get involved in this very important subject. Here's how you and your church can be salt and light in this situation:

- Pray
- Implement, maintain, and update safe church child protection policies.
- Require leaders in the church to complete boundary and trauma training.
- Take a special offering for your local domestic violence or sexual assault organizations.
- During the months of April (Sexual Assault Awareness) and October (Domestic Violence Awareness) encourage your church to participate in some way whether it be providing services to these organizations, having a sermon series, etc.
- Provide resources for your congregation to raise awareness and be educated.
- If you see something, say something! You can help stop someone from becoming a victim.

BEFORE I WROTE THIS SENTENCE, I prayed for you. I trust you will be used mightily by God in this matter.

DAY TWENTY

GENESIS 35:1 - 36:43

"The greatest legacy one can pass on to one's children and grandchildren is not money or other material things accumulated in one's life, but rather a legacy of character and faith." - Billy Graham (1918 - 2018)

∾

JACOB RETURNS TO BETHEL

Today's passage opens with God's command to Jacob to fulfill the vow he made about 30 years earlier to go back to Bethel (Gen. 28:20 – 22) and we see God mentioned 10x in this chapter. It's like a drink of refreshingly cold water in the middle of a hot desert when you come back to the Lord after being so spiritually dry like Jacob and his family were. It's as if Jacob found his "big-boy pants", put them on, and decided to be the spiritual leader of the home once again. Before the covenant family returns to their place of worship in Bethel, Jacob ordered that the idols of their household be removed, purify themselves, and even change their garments symbolizing cleansed lives. The lesson for us is that salvation is the first step towards sanctification. Just because we've been saved by Christ doesn't mean we have an intimate, passionate, lively, and tangible relationship with Him. We must remove those things in our household that influence us towards ungodliness, pursue purity in our minds, and clothe ourselves in practical holiness in order to have a rich connection with our Savior.

Israel (AKA – Jacob) is now where he needs to be; back in Bethel. For a moment I would like to give special attention to the drink offering mentioned in Genesis 35:14. The drink offering was a supplemental offering to the regular animal sacrifices and was poured on the altar as the sacrifice was burning (Exodus 29:40 – 41; Number 6:17). This would ultimately become symbolic of dedication as the believer's life would be poured out for the Lord (2ⁿᵈ Samuel 23:16). Paul considered the pouring out of his life before God to be like a drink offering on God's altar (Philippians 2:17; 2ⁿᵈ Timothy 4:6). It's the daily goal of every Christian to be a drink offering; to pour out to others in service what God has poured into us.

JACOB'S FAMILY

Genesis 35:16 – 29 gives us a bird's eye view of Jacob's family. As the covenant family journeyed South from Bethel back to Hebron, Rachel died in childbirth. She named the child Ben-Oni (son of my sorrow), but Jacob named him Benjamin (son of my right hand). There is a glimpse of Christ here because the Son of God would become a man well acquainted with sorrow (Isaiah 53) before returning back to the Father to forever sit at His right hand (Romans 8:34). Regarding Rachel's death, some have asked the question, "Why wasn't she buried with Abraham, Sarah, Isaac, Rebekah, and Leah in Hebron?" This is not definitive, but I strongly believe that God's desire was for Jacob to marry Leah. It was through Leah that the line of the priests (Levi) and the line of kings (Judah) by whom Jesus would fulfill both High Priest and King according to the order of Melchizedek would come from. Perhaps Jacob realized this as he matured and chose to honor her, but not have her buried with his ancestors, and Leah (Genesis 49:31).

As we continue our adventure in Genesis together, we will become more familiar with Israel's 12 sons, but one thing is for certain; this is one messed up family. If you think you have a dysfunctional family with all of your drama, then you're in good company. If God can use people like this, then I firmly believe He can use people like us. Just remember, the Savior of the world came *from* the very types of people He would save.

ESAU'S FAMILY

Genesis 36 is devoted to the descendants of Esau, who dwelt in the land of Edom, which is Southwest of the Dead Sea. This chapter fulfills the prophecy made in Genesis 25:23 that Esau would be the head of a nation and this chapter is essentially closing the record of Esau before we continue to the plan of redemption through the covenant family of Israel. Before we close the record of the nation of Edom, here are four important points regarding them:

- Several prophets spoke out against Edom: Jeremiah (Jer.49:17-18), Ezekiel (Ezek.25:12–14), Malachi (Mal.1:1-4), and most of Obadiah.
- When the Israelites were traveling to the Promised Land, the Edomites did not allow them to pass through their land (Num.20:21) which discouraged the Israelis (Num.21:4).
- In the days of King Saul, Edom was subject to Israel (1st Sam.14:47) and later with King David (2nd Sam.8:14), but later in the days of King Joram, the Edomites

rebelled and fulfilled the prophecy of Isaac in Genesis 27:40.

- When Greek became the common language during the time of the Maccabees, the Edomites began to be called Idumaeans and from the Idumaeans came Herod the Great. After the death of the 5 Herods, the Edomites disappeared from history thus fulfilling the prophecy of God in Ezekiel 35:15.

Though these men have conquered much land, set up governments, had societal status, and acquired much wealth; these are dead men. The question we need to ask in some way is not, "Are you successful?" but, "Are you alive?" Jesus said it best in Matthew 16:26, "What good will it be for someone to gain the whole world, yet forfeit their soul?" God cares infinitely more for your spiritual health than your physical or financial health. Not only do we need to be alive in Christ and publicly demonstrate that, but call others to do the same.

DEEPER THAN THAT, we must leave a legacy of godliness and not worldliness.

LET'S PRAY, *"Dear God, I'm amazed at Your patience and grace towards me. I am so undeserving to even be alive, let alone be saved and used by You to advance Your glorious name into all the world. Thank You for the opportunity to know, love, and serve You. Please help me to see the danger of disobedience and the blessing of obedience in order to build and leave behind a godly legacy for You to use. I ask this in the name of Jesus. Amen."*

∽

ACTION POINT

One of the big picture topics of today's passage is that of leaving a legacy. When you pass from this life into the next, how will you be remembered and how will your life continually be making an impact when you're gone? Today's Action Point is to consider leaving a legacy in the following four areas:

Spiritual - When I die, I don't want to be remembered for my accomplishments, I want to be remembered simply as someone who loved and pointed people to Christ. Live a life in God's word, prayer, and aggressively pursuing holiness as a byproduct of your worship to God.

Family - There have been decisions my wife and I have made where we said "no" to certain things in order to say "yes" to our family. Prioritize your family as your first ministry. Spend quality and quantity of time with them, laugh, and make cherished memories to the best of your ability.

Work - Outperform everyone while empowering them to do better. Lead from the front while helping those behind you move beyond their expectations. Humbly be the best by letting your results speak for themselves. Improve and grow your organization; don't simply maintain it and try to survive. Let your business, school, and workplace environment see your good works and glorify your Father in Heaven (Matthew 5:16).

Financial - Proverbs 13:22 says, "A good person leaves an inheritance for their children's children..." Get on a biblical financial plan to get out of debt, stay out of debt, build wealth, and give not only to Kingdom work, but to leave behind an inheritance to your kids and grandkids. Teach your family biblical money management to go farther and faster than you ever did.

YOUR LIFE IS the dash in between two numbers on a tombstone. How are you going to spend it?

DAY TWENTY-ONE

GENESIS 37:1 - 36

"While other worldviews lead us to sit in the midst of life's joys, foreseeing the coming sorrows, Christianity empowers its people to sit in the midst of this world's sorrows, tasting the coming joy." - Timothy Keller, Pastor & Author

JOSEPH TAKES CENTER STAGE

As we step into Genesis 37 together we now see Joseph take center stage. If God devoted 14 chapters primarily to 1 character, then we should pay close attention. Throughout this chapter we find hatred (Vs.1-4), envy (Vs.5-11), investigation (Vs.12-17), conspiracy (Vs.18-24), indifference (Vs.23-28), and deception (Vs.29-36).

DREAMS & VISIONS

Due to the fact dreams and visions are not only in our passage today, but throughout Scripture, I would like us to see the many instances they are used and discuss whether or not God still uses them today.

Old Testament Dreams and Visions

- *Abraham* (Genesis 15:1): God used a vision to restate the Abrahamic Covenant,
- *Abimelech* (Genesis 20:1 - 7): Abimelech took Sarah into his harem, but God sent him a dream telling him not to touch Sarah because she was Abraham's wife. This was God was protecting the covenant line.
- *Jacob* (Genesis 28:10 - 17): He had his famous dream of a ladder reaching to heaven on which angels ascended and descended; referencing the Messiah to come. In this dream Jacob received God's promise that Abraham's blessing would be carried on through him.
- *Joseph* (Genesis 37:1 - 11): Joseph is one of the most famous dreamers and dream-interpreters, in the Bible.
- *Pharaoh's cupbearer and baker* (Genesis 40): While in prison Joseph interpreted some dreams of Pharaoh's cupbearer and baker. With God's guidance, he explained that the cupbearer would return to Pharaoh's service, but the baker would be killed.
- *Pharaoh* (Genesis 41): Two years later, Pharaoh himself had a dream which Joseph interpreted. God's purpose was to raise Joseph to second-in-command over Egypt in order to save the Egyptians and Israelites from a horrible famine.
- *Samuel* (1st Samuel 3): Samuel had his first vision as a young boy. God told him that judgment was coming upon the sons of Samuel's mentor, Eli. The young Samuel was faithful to relay the information.
- *The Midianite and Amalekite armies* (Judges 7:12 - 15): The pagan enemies of Israel had a divinely inspired dream. God told Gideon to sneak into the enemy camp

at night, and there in the outposts of the camp, Gideon overheard an enemy soldier relate a dream he had just had. The interpretation, from another enemy soldier, mentioned Gideon by name and predicted that Israel would win the battle. Gideon was greatly encouraged by this.

- *Solomon* (1st Kings 3:5): It was in a dream that God gave Solomon the famous offer: "Ask what you wish Me to give you." Solomon chose wisdom.
- *Daniel* (Daniel 2:4): As He had done for Joseph, God placed Daniel in a position of power and influence by allowing him to interpret a foreign ruler's dream. Daniel himself had many dreams and visions, mostly related to future kingdoms of the world, the nation of Israel, and the Messiah.

New Testament Dreams & Visions

- *Zacharias* (Luke 1:5 - 23): God used a vision to tell Zacharias, an old priest, that he would soon have an important son. Not long after, Zacharias and his wife, Elizabeth, had John the Baptist.
- *Joseph* (Matthew 1:20; 2:13): God sent an angel to him in a dream, convincing him that the pregnancy was of God. After Jesus was born, God sent two more dreams, one to tell Joseph to take his family to Egypt so Herod could not kill Jesus and another to tell him Herod was dead and that he could return home.
- *Pilate's wife* (Matthew 27:19): During Jesus' trial, Pilate's wife sent an urgent message to the governor encouraging him to free Jesus. Her message was prompted by a dream she had—a nightmare, really— that convinced her that Jesus was innocent and that Pilate should have nothing to do with His case.

- *Ananias* (Acts 9:10): God gave Ananias a vision and reassurance to go to Saul.
- *Cornelius* (Acts 10:1 - 6): In his vision, Cornelius saw an angel who told him where to find Simon Peter and to send for him and listen to his message.
- *Peter* (Acts 10:9 - 15): While Peter was praying on the rooftop of a house in Joppa, God gave him a vision of animals lowered in something like a sheet.
- *Paul*: Paul had several visions in his missionary career. One sent him to preach in Macedonia (Acts 16:9 - 10). Another encouraged him to keep preaching in Corinth (Acts 18:9 - 11). God also gave him a vision of heaven (2nd Corinthians 12:1 - 6).
- *John* (Revelation): Nearly the entire book of Revelation is a vision John had while exiled on the island of Patmos. John's vision explains in more detail some of the events that God had shown Daniel.

It's clear that Scripture teaches dreams and visions were one of God's many ways of communicating and there is nothing to indicate He still doesn't communicate that way today. However, God's primary communication is through the Bible, and whatever dreams or visions we may have, must be filtered through the truthfulness of His word to test if it is truly from Him.

SHEPHERD TO SLAVE OF EGYPT

The majority of our passage today speaks of the shepherd Joseph, son of Jacob, being hated and sold into slavery by his brothers. Little did their father Jacob know that this would be the last time he would see his son Joseph for over 20 years. As we continue together we'll see that this horrible act will plague Joseph's brothers for many years (Gen. 42:21 – 22). This is an important reminder that our sins have lasting consequences; either externally or internally in our own conscience. Can you imagine what day-to-day family life must've been like after this?

As difficult as it may sound, God ordained and predestined Joseph to go through this suffering in order to make his way to Egypt for reasons we will see later. It was not that God caused these men to sin; rather, He used their imperfect decisions to bring about His perfect will. Though Joseph had not read Romans 8:28, he was a living example of that truth. Little did he know, that one day, he would speak the words of Genesis 50:20, "... you meant evil against me, but God meant it for good..."

HERE'S where this has relevancy for us. No matter what level of tragedy you're going through, God will not waste any experiences. He is in the business of turning trials into triumphs. My hope is that comfort fills and overflows your heart because you hold tightly to the truth that God will use your difficult situation for your good and His glory. That's a promise and God doesn't break His promises.

LET'S PRAY, *"Dear God, thank You for Your word where I can find truth, see You working through Your people, and understanding how You want to work in my life. You see my suffering right now and I ask that You would give me Your peace that goes beyond understanding. I'm trusting that You are going to use this situation to make me more like Jesus and bring glory to Yourself. Please help me to lead by example to have joy through trials so that others can be encouraged to look to You at all times, but especially in hard times. I ask this in the name of Jesus. Amen."*

~

ACTION POINT

Today's Action Point is to "...count it all joy when you fall into various trials" (James 1:2). Joseph suffered severely at the hands of others and yet maintained a strong walk with the Lord; a good example for us.

God is most glorified in us when we are most satisfied in Him and least glorified in us when we are least satisfied in Him. Think about whatever hardship you're going through right now and ask yourself, "Are my thoughts and actions demonstrating that I'm satisfied in my Savior or am I complaining and having a bad attitude?"

Personally, this is what I tell myself when I'm going through a rough time, "At least I'm not going to Hell." It's true! No matter what irritating, agonizing, and drawn-out hardship I'm going through, it will never come close to the suffering of eternal separation from God under His wrath.

CHOOSE JOY, my friend. As a child of God, there is always reason to smile.

DAY TWENTY-TWO

GENESIS 38:1 - 30

"<big>O</big>n occasion a Christian will wander away from the fellowship of other believers and find himself ensnared by sin through ignorance or willful disobedience. It then becomes necessary for the church, and particularly its shepherds, to actively seek the repentance and restoration of that Christian." - John MacArthur, Pastor & Author

INTRO TO TRAGEDY

We've now seen another tragedy within the covenant line.

Some have asked the question, "When did this event occur?" Well, Joseph was 17 when he was sold into slavery, and 30 when he became 2nd in command of Egypt, which gives us 13 years. When you add the 7 years of plenty and the 2 years of famine, you have 22 years before Joseph was reconciled to his brothers. That's plenty of time for Judah to marry, have 3 sons, bury 2 sons and a wife, and get involved with Tamar. Also, if this event happened before Joseph was sold, then that gives even more time.

As we move forward, let's answer the question, "Why is this event recorded?" I would like to propose the following 4 reasons: 1) History, 2) Morality, 3) Covenant Community, and 4) Grace.

HISTORY

One of the major purposes of Genesis is to record the origin and development of the family of Jacob, the founder of the 12 tribes of Israel. The Israelites went down to Egypt a large family, then 430 years later, they came out a large nation. Since the tribe of Judah is the royal line from which the Messiah would come , anything related to Judah is vital to both Genesis and God's plan of redemption.

Also, without this chapter, we wouldn't know why Tamar and Perez are in our Savior's genealogy (Matthew 1:3). Perez was an ancestor of King David (Ruth 4:18 - 22) and therefore an ancestor of Jesus the Messiah. Let me show you, please turn to 1st Chronicles 2:3 - 15. We see the lineage go from Judah, to Perez, to Hezron, to Ram, to Nashon, to Boaz, to Obed, to Jesse, and then David. This is a beautiful example of God taking a tragedy and turning it into a triumph!

MORALITY

This chapter has some practical life lessons as well. Notice Judah's hasty and self-righteous rebuke in Vs.24. This highlights the truth of Romans 1:28 that the more we sin, the more we are given over to a debased or seared mind. When that happens, we are no longer sensitive to our own sin, but quick to point it out in others. We need to lead by example in following Jesus publicly and privately before exhorting others to do so.

There's also a dramatic contrast between Judah and Joseph. Joseph refused to compromise himself with Potiphar's wife while Judah not only married a pagan woman, but also had a one-night stand with his daughter-in-law whom he thought was a prostitute.

Throughout the covenant family so far there has been this theme of deception. Abraham lied about his wife, Isaac did the same, Jacob used goat hair to deceive his father Isaac, Joseph's brothers used a garment to deceive their father Jacob; now, Tamar used a garment to deceive Judah! The critical lesson is this. By God's power, we need to be the stop to our habitual family sins. The generational crazy cycle must be broken.

COVENANT COMMUNITY

Judah got himself into trouble when he began spending more time with the Canaanites than with the covenant family. Like Samson, he saw a woman he liked and married her without God's approval (Judges 14). For Christians today, we need to stay close to our New Covenant family more than our own Canaanite world; those who would entice us away from the Lord.

GRACE

Throughout the entire historical record of Genesis we see the grace of God amplified under horrific situations and His sovereign hand working in the background. The men and women of the covenant family were obviously not perfect, sometimes deliberately disobedient, but God still used them to accomplish His purposes.

Please take some time to read 1st Corinthians 1:26 - 31. In light of that passage and Genesis 38, please let me give you some words of encouragement. Don't believe the lies of demons or your flesh that, as a Christian, you're not good enough, pure enough, or talented enough, because if God can use the incredibly dysfunctional people of Genesis, then He can use people like us to accomplish His will and advance His kingdom. It's time for us to rest in that.

LET'S PRAY, *"Dear God, thank You for being slow to anger, rich in mercy, and quick to forgive. Thank You that You're the God of new beginnings. Thank You for Your ability to take horrible situations and make something beautiful out of them. I'm grateful that when I mess up so many times You are still willing to heal me, transform me, and use me for Your greater plan. Please help me to receive discipline from You and my spiritual leaders. Please help me to lovingly correct my brothers and sisters so we can all mature together. I ask this in the name of Jesus. Amen."*

ACTION POINT

The event we read about today regarding Judah and Tamar did not happen all of a sudden. It was the result of unchecked sinful lifestyles over a long period of time. In order to prevent situations like this from happening in our own personal lives or churches, it is important that we follow the teaching of Jesus in Matthew 18:15 - 17 by implementing Church Discipline. Therefore, your Action Point for today is to follow Jesus' four step method to correcting Christians with truth in love:

1. **One-on-one** - Don't talk to your friends, parents, pastor or anyone else about the situation; rather, truthfully and lovingly confront the sinning Christian. If unsuccessful, proceed to step two.
2. **Bring one or two others** - These are to be mature believers who are aware of the situation and present for accountability. If unsuccessful, proceed to step three.

3. **Bring the situation to church elders** - The pastor(s) of the fellowship the sinning Christian attends are now to step in and correct. If unsuccessful, proceed to step four.

4. **Excommunication** - If the sinning Christian has been repeatedly confronted and is continually unrepentant, then for the health of the local church, that person is to be removed from the fellowship until they repent and the church leaders find it appropriate to let the individual return. Important passages on this topic are 1st Corinthians 5:1 - 13; 2nd Thessalonians 3:14; Romans 16:17; Titus 3:10; 2nd Timothy 3:1 - 5.

DUE TO THE fact that the topic of Church Discipline is so important and deserves much more attention, I highly recommend the book "Church Discipline: How the Church Protects the Name of Jesus" by Jonathan Leeman.

AS A PASTOR, this is a consistent part of my duty to fight for the purity, health, and growth of God's Church. However, all of God's people are called to humbly correct one another. When our local churches have a healthy culture of maintaining a biblical standard of character and conduct then we will powerfully move forward in a God-honoring direction.

DAY TWENTY-THREE

GENESIS 39:1 - 23

"First, chastity is not the only, or even the most important, aspect of Christian discipleship. Indeed, even to think about, say, chastity, tithing, and prayer as wholly discreet, distinct activities is to miss the point — for the gospel is not an invitation to compartmentalized living. It is, instead, an engagement in love. The questions we Christians should ask are not, "Do I have the energy to deal with chastity or tithing this week?" but, "What is the whole duty of man? What does it mean to be wholly converted?" - Lauren Winner, Historian & Author

SUPERVISOR OF POTIPHAR'S HOUSE

The phrase, "the LORD was with Joseph" is a theme throughout Joseph's life and that same phrase applies to every one of God's children today. The pagan Egyptian Potiphar knew nothing of the God of Joseph and yet he saw something different in this slave; his character, his work ethic, and his speech set him apart from everyone else. Joseph was a faithful administrator as a shepherd under his father Jacob, and now, God is blessing Joseph's faithfulness by granting him greater responsibility. This is an Old Testament example of a New Testament truth where Jesus said, "Whoever can be trusted with very little can also be trusted in much..." (Luke 16:10). What are your responsibilities right now? Do you want a promotion at work, a bigger ministry, excel academically or athletically, etc.? Then you must work with excellence now before God will grant you greater responsibilities later.

SUPERVISOR OF PHARAOH'S PRISONERS

After being unjustly accused, innocent Joseph now finds himself imprisoned beside the criminals of Egypt. Living an average life in the ancient world was difficult enough, but to be put in the horrendous conditions Joseph was in would cause anyone to ask the question, "Why?". This is when people ask, "Why do bad things happen to good people?" It's important to clarify something here. There was only one time bad things happened to a good person and His name is Jesus. No one is essentially good by nature except God (Romans 3:10-12).

The faster we apply this truth, the more content we will be: God never called us to understand all things, He simply called us to trust Him in all things (Proverbs 3:5).

Joseph must've had an extraordinary character to gain the trust of the prison guard, so much so that he became the supervisor of the prisoners while being a prisoner himself! God had been sharpening Joseph's administrative skills from being a shepherd, to overseer of Potiphar's house, and now the supervisor of prisoners. As Joseph's story progresses, we'll see this was all to prepare him for even greater responsibility in the future. How beautiful it is that God doesn't waste any experiences. Everything the Lord has you doing today is to prepare you for tomorrow. All of the battles you fight today are making you stronger for tomorrow.

SEXUAL PURITY

The "elephant in the room" of today's passage is the topic of sexual purity. Joseph is an Old Testament example of the New Testament truth found in 2nd Timothy 2:22 where Paul encourages the young pastor Timothy to "flee youthful lusts". Let's think about the situation here. Joseph is referred to as handsome, which likely came from his mother Rachel, and it's noteworthy to mention that the Bible calls only two other men "good-looking" which is David (1st Samuel 16:12) and his third son Absalom (2nd Samuel 14:25). With that being said, let's think about how strong this sexual temptation would have been. First of all, Joseph is physically attractive, he's likely in his 20's which means raging hormones, no doubt he is a virgin, it would be normal for him to have bitterness being a slave and want to spite the Egyptians by laying with Potiphar's wife, and most likely she would have been physically attractive to Joseph's eyes also. However, notice Joseph's response in Genesis 39:9. He was aware of God's presence and already predetermined in his mind to not commit sexual immorality. King David said something similar almost 1,000 years later in Psalm 51:10 after committing adultery with Bathsheba and having her husband Uriah murdered. I encourage you to take a moment and read David's words.

This reminds me of a quote from Charles Spurgeon which I think is appropriate as we close today's passage and get ready for our Action Point. Spurgeon said, "When I regarded God as a tyrant, I thought sin a trifle, but when I knew him to be my Father, then I mourned that I could ever have kicked against Him. When I thought that God was hard, I found it easy to sin, but when I found God so kind, so good, so overflowing with compassion, I smote upon my breast to think that I could ever have rebelled against the one who loved me so, and sought my good."

· · ·

THE WORLD IS INCREASINGLY BECOMING over-sexualized and it is the duty of God's people to not only pursue sexual purity as individuals, but raise the sexual standard in the Church. If God's Bride is not pursuing sexual purity and walking in the light, then how can we expect to have an impact on those walking in darkness? The Church must disciple Christians in the area of sexuality, or else, the world will.

LET'S PRAY, *"Dear God, You are the very source of love and romance. You created sex to be enjoyed in the context of biblical marriage. Please forgive me for the times my thoughts and actions have wandered into sexual immorality. Please help me to pursue sexual purity and to call Your people to do the same so we can glorify You and have a greater impact on those walking in darkness. I ask this in the name of Jesus. Amen."*

∾

ACTION POINT

Joseph exemplified sexual purity in today's passage; therefore, your Action Point today is to either begin implementing or strengthen your pursuit of sexual purity while calling fellow Christians to do the same.

The following is a list of things I personally do to keep me walking victoriously in this area:

- **Mindset**: I strive to maintain my passion for Christ to always be greater than my passion for sin. This is done through the foundational consistent practices of reading Scripture, prayer, and fasting.
- **Growth**: I invest into myself by consuming resources

on marriage and Christian growth by reading books, listening to podcasts, etc.

- **Accountable**: I have people in my life, known as "Accountability Partners" to ask me the tough questions on life, marriage, and ministry. These are men I can depend on for wise counsel, prayer, or just a listening ear.
- **Practical**: My wife has access to all of my devices and information. I choose to rarely use social media because inappropriate or explicit content is too easily seen. I have Covenant Eyes installed on my devices and another piece of equipment that filters everyone's internet usage at home. As I go through my day I make the conscious intentional decision to turn my eyes away from sensually dressed women.
- **Ministry**: Our church has a variety of practices and policies in place to keep staff, volunteers, minors, and anyone else on the property safe from sexual immorality, misconduct, or allegations.

TOO MANY OF our brothers and sisters in Christ have been destroyed by sexual immorality. Don't be one of them. Fight for purity. Raise the standard in your personal life, in your church, and in your community. We have the power of God and all the tools we need to win this fight. So let's do it.

DAY TWENTY-FOUR

GENESIS 40:1 - 23

"When the Bible speaks of patience it speaks of it as a virtue that goes far beyond the mere ability to await some future gain. It involves more than the rest or peace of the soul that trusts in God's perfect timing. The patience that is in view here focuses more on interpersonal relationships with other people. It is the patience of longsuffering and of forbearing in the midst of personal injury. This is the most difficult patience of all." - R.C. Sproul, Pastor & Theologian (1939 - 2017)

JOSEPH, BUTLER, AND BAKER

The positions of being chief butler and chief baker were high offices. The butler, or cupbearer, was in charge of Pharaoh's drinks and the baker, or chef, was in charge of Pharaoh's food. Some believe these men were involved in a plot to poison the Pharaoh. Regardless of why they were sent to prison, the God-ordained reason of why they were there was to meet Joseph. Notice Joseph's response to these men in verse 4 where it says "he served them". Though Joseph was in a position of authority over the prisoners, he did not use his authority to get his own will accomplished; rather, he used his authority to serve those whom he oversaw. This is so important for you as a leader, to use your authority and influence to help, lift up, and serve those around you.

GENESIS 40:5 – 7 is a small window into Joseph's heart. If we were unjustly imprisoned in a horrible environment, would we be quick to not only notice the hardship of others, but be quick to meet their needs? A true test of your spiritual maturity is how joyfully you serve while suffering. No doubt it's the default mode for humans to complain, have a bad attitude, and be short-tempered when life is difficult, but we must fight against that. The glory of God and the well-being of others is more important than my selfish impulses.

As THE BUTLER and baker begin to open up about their dreams Joseph responds rhetorically, "Do not interpretations belong to God?" This conversation shows us that Joseph acknowledges where the gift of interpretation comes from; you cannot take a class to learn it nor can you find the answers within yourself, but the interpretation is from God. It's shameful when God does a miraculous work in someone's heart, in a family, or a church and some individual tries to take credit for it. We also learn from Joseph's conversation with these men that he was naturally evan-gelistic. Just as he mentioned God with Potiphar (Genesis 39:3) and his wife (Genesis 39:9), so he does here with these prisoners. I'm concerned that many Christians have lost what it means to be His witnesses to the ends of the Earth (Acts 1:8); to constantly seek ways to influence those around them towards the Kingdom of God. Let's lead by example like Joseph to intentionally represent Christ appropriately and speak of Him constantly.

SEER OF DREAMS

So far, we've seen Joseph, son of Jacob, go from shepherd, to slave, to supervisor of Potiphar's house, to supervisor of Pharaoh's prisoners, and now to a seer. God gave Joseph insight to interpret and see the dreams as God sees them. As Joseph gave the butler the interpretation, he used it as an opportunity to try and get himself out of prison. Some would say this was not an act of faith; however, just because something is practical does not mean it is not spiritual. Let me share a quick story to illustrate. A man out at sea became shipwrecked and prayed for God to save him. A lifeboat comes, but he rejects the help. A helicopter comes, but he rejects the help. He ends up dying of dehydration, gets to heaven, asks God angrily why He didn't save him, and God says, "I tried with the lifeboat and helicopter." The man reply's with, "...Oh." All that to be said, faith does not exclude action. We must pray as if everything depends on Him and work as if everything depends on us.

When Joseph turned to the baker and gave him his interpretation, I'm sure that's not the message he was wanting to hear. This makes me think of how many people want to preach the butler message, but not the baker message. Some Christians only want people to feel good instead of speaking the hard truths of the Bible into their lives. The big picture is that the culture we live in is a result of the things we do and the things we don't do. The environment we create is a result of what we say and what we don't say. This principle can be applied to you personally, to your family dynamics, your church culture, and your community. Speak truth regardless if it's unpopular or uncomfortable. When you go to meet God, you'll be glad you did.

PATIENCE

At the end of our passage today we find the soul crushing phrase, "… the chief butler did not remember Joseph, but forgot him." Can you imagine Joseph's anticipation?! He was probably telling himself, "Only a few more days and I'll be out of here." Then a few days became weeks, became months, and then 2 years! Why did God allow this? Because Joseph is going to need more than administrative skill to accomplish what God wants him to accomplish; he is going to need mental strength and endurance. This is so applicable for us today. So many people overestimate what they can do in the short-term and underestimate what they can do in the long-term. In the big picture, God uses the struggle to sanctify us, He uses the chaos to conform us into the image of His Son. My friend, push through the pain of what you're going through. There are people who want to cheer you on if you let them in on what's happening. Get comfortable with being uncomfortable because that is the way of Jesus. Dig deep. Press further. Don't give up.

LET'S PRAY, *"Dear God, thank You for being with me on the mountain tops and in the valleys; in the good times and the bad. Help me to be patient. Help me to learn what it means to struggle joyfully. I want to glorify You by getting better, not bitter. As I do, please help me to show others to do the same. I ask this in the name of Jesus. Amen."*

∾

ACTION POINT

In light of our passage today, and what happened to Joseph, your Action Point today is to strengthen your patience. I don't know what you're going through, but I do know that those whom God greatly uses He first greatly breaks and prepares. It's time for God to break us of our impatience and prepare us for greater acts of service. There are many strategic and tactical ways to mature in this area, but here are three concepts that have helped me and I hope also help you to fulfill your Action Point and strengthen your patience:

- **Decree** - First of all, patience is a decree, it is commanded by God for His people, (Eph. 4:2; Rom. 12:12; Col. 3:12) and best exemplified by Himself (1st Tim. 1:16; 2nd Pet. 3:9; Rom. 15:5). Our fulfillment of patience must not be accomplished out of obligation, chore, or begrudgingly; rather, out of love, adoration, and joy. Patience is an act of worship. On a personal note, I think of how much God has been patient with me, and then think, "How can I not be patient towards this person or situation?"

- **Destination** - Keep your "why" in mind and your goal in sight. Good leaders always lead their people with the *why* before they lead with the *what*. Whether you are pursuing personal, relational, academic, career, financial, or ministerial goals, you will need to be patient along the way and a great way to stay the course is by keeping those goals in mind. Make them visual, set reminders for yourself in your environment for why you do what you do. Before we lead others we must first lead ourselves.

- **Discipline** - Discipline is a key to progress. Discipline is a skill, and like all skills, it can be learned, strengthened, and matured. Your ability to focus, not just on being patient, but on any important task, is a defining feature that will set you apart from those around you. It will not be easy, but it will be worth it. For me, one passion must overcome another passion. My passion to honor

God by being patient must overcome my passion to sinfully honor myself by being impatient. I must be aggressive, intense, and intentional in the way I discipline myself towards patience and all other important matters.

DAY TWENTY-FIVE

GENESIS 41:1 - 57

" **C**enteredness is difficult to describe and impossible to miss. So, what makes a centered leader? First, they are guided by values, driven by purpose, and obsessed with mission. You'll find that centered leaders are grounded, aware, secure, and consistent."
- Craig Groeschel, Pastor & Author

THE BIBLE IS FILLED with the sovereignty of God and this chapter is a shining example of how He moves among the affairs of mankind.

GOD GAVE...

... Pharaoh two dreams. One of the major Egyptian goddesses was named Hathor and was represented by the cow. Hathor was the goddess of sky, love, beauty, joy, motherhood, foreign lands, mining, music, and fertility. Pharaoh is troubled because he sees the Egyptian economy, their way of life, potentially coming to an end, and he is finding no answers among his current resources.

GOD REMINDED...

... the Cupbearer about Joseph. It was time for Joseph to be given a throne; he was ready after all of his suffering and preparation. However, for a moment, think about what it was like in this very moment for Joseph. It was just another day in prison with seemingly no hope. How many of us would get depressed, walk away from our faithfulness to God, and live in bitterness? My friend, there are times in your journey that you will want to walk away from Christ because of your crisis, but you must not allow your feelings to overrule the facts. The fact is God is alive, He is working behind the scenes of your life, and He is not wasting any of your experiences. He is preparing you for more. Lean into the struggle; learn, grow, and be trained by it.

GOD LED...

... Pharaoh to summon Joseph. Pharaoh, the most powerful man on the Earth at this time and who is even worshipped as a god by his people, is now coming to this Hebrew slave prisoner for answers. So who is really the most powerful man in this situation? The one with truth. The same is true today; the most truthful are the most powerful. Now, whether or not the world submits to that truth is a different story. When your non-Christian friends, family, coworkers, and strangers are not finding adequate answers to their problems, who will they go to? They will turn to you because they know there is something you have that they don't; truth.

Notice what Joseph does when summoned by Pharaoh; he simply gives the interpretation and the solution, but does not promote himself. How quickly would we not only give the interpretation, the solution, and then try to promote ourselves out of prison as the one to execute the plan? The words of Jesus ring true in Matthew 23:12, "And whoever exalts himself shall be humbled, and he who humbles himself will be exalted." Joseph led by example in this and we ought to follow in his steps.

Little did Joseph know that God had been preparing him since the day he was born to step into a position he would never have dreamed possible. The same God who did this for Joseph wants to do the same to you; He wants to go above and beyond in your life. Humble yourself to Him, and in His timing, He will lift you up.

GOD MOVED...

... Pharaoh to choose Joseph. When times of famine sweep the land the world needs men and women filled with the Spirit of God to exercise His wisdom in times of trouble. Why does God allow such darkness during the days of Joseph and during our time? So that you, His people, will allow His light to shine bright in the darkness. When you see the problems of your culture, I encourage you to see opportunity.

GOD USED...

... Joseph to provide food for the surrounding lands. If God promised to Joseph at age 17 through a dream that he would rule the known world, why didn't God fulfill it then? Because God knew that if he was 2nd in command of Egypt at age 17, Joseph would have no practical competency, perhaps abuse his authority, and ultimately misrepresent the Lord. God is wise in delaying many opportunities to you because He knows you need preparation first. One of the detrimental mindsets of some people is that they want the top positions, but don't want the necessary work, perseverance, and character to get there.

GOD MADE...

...Joseph into the leader the world needed. Here's a thought as we get ready to finish together: Joseph is arguably the only worshipper in Egypt of the one true God. How quickly would our character break without any church community, accountability, or Christian friendships? How many of us would maintain a strong, impenetrable, relationship to Christ without the support of His people? My hope and prayer for you is not that you would faithfully walk with Jesus independently from His people, but that you could if necessary.

There is so much to be said about Joseph's "rags to riches" story, but one of the biblically practical truths I would like us to extract from our passage today is that of **leadership**. Joseph was a centered leader. Everyone is a leader because everyone has influence. Today, let's strive to improve our leadership because when the leader gets better, everyone gets better.

LET'S PRAY, *"Dear God, thank You for Your wisdom. Thank You for knowing what is best for me and creating opportunities for that to be fulfilled. Please help me to follow Joseph's example by having an immovable character in the midst of darkness and an unstoppable leadership in the face of seemingly insurmountable problems. I ask this in the name of Jesus. Amen."*

∼

ACTION POINT

Strong Christian Leadership is an absolute essential in both the Church and the world. Therefore, because you are a leader, your Action Point for today is to either begin, or continue, consistently sharpening your leadership skills by consuming and applying quality Christian leadership resources. At the time of this writing, here are four people and resources that have personally impacted my leadership and I trust will be valuable to you as well:

- Craig Groeschel's Leadership Podcast
- John Maxwell's Leadership Podcast
- Andy Stanley's Leadership Podcast
- The book Spiritual Leadership by Oswald Sanders

I personally consume a lot of content through audio, but regardless of your preference, keep pursuing knowledge, personal growth, spiritual maturity, and the sharpening of your leadership. Read books, listen to podcasts, interview Christian leaders, attend conferences, and intentionally seek to improve yourself, by the power of God, daily.

I WANT to share a reminder at this point that I am committed to being your servant and I want to help you be all that God wants you to be; to be the best version of yourself. With that being said, feel free to contact me directly if you have specific questions, want to talk, or if there is anything I can I help you with. Now, as the Lord is leading you, go and lead others for His glory.

DAY TWENTY-SIX

GENESIS 42:1 - 45:15

"Four of the Ten Commandments deal with our relationship to God while the other six deal with our relationships with people. But all ten are about relationships." - Rick Warren, Pastor & Author

THE FIRST TEST

In Genesis 42 we see the first encounter between Joseph and his brothers in at least 20 years. The prophecy that God gave to Joseph through a dream of his brothers bowing down to him is now fulfilled (Genesis 37:5-8). Joseph's brother's do not recognize his appearance or voice because a lot has changed in 20 years. With that being said, Joseph needs to test his brothers to see if they have changed also; not externally, but internally. As we will see later in Genesis, Joseph wants a restored relationship with his brothers, but he needs to see if they have repented of their former ways.

The first test Joseph administers is jailing his brothers for 3 days, keeping Simeon while the rest get their youngest brother Benjamin, and returning their money. Now, what was the purpose of this first test? While in jail, Joseph wanted to see what kind of conversation would take place, and it was one of acknowledging unconfessed sin (Genesis 42:21-23). The purpose of keeping Simeon was to see if they were going to leave him just like they left Joseph in the pit. The purpose of Joseph returning their money was to see if they were going to be honest and return it back. The purpose of wanting to see Benjamin was to see if they treated him as badly as they treated Joseph.

It's important to note at this point that God commands us to forgive (Ephesians 4:32), and by His power, we can. However, forgiveness does not include reconciliation because that is a two-way street. Joseph can forgive his brothers, but that does not immediately mean they are reconciled together to a healthy relationship. You can forgive those who have hurt, neglected, and abused you, but that does not mean you have a reconciled relationship with them, but you can. Are you and that person willing to go through the necessary work to honor God in this way? We'll touch on that in just a bit.

THE SECOND TEST

In Genesis 43 we see Joseph's second test being administered; showing favoritism towards the youngest brother, Benjamin, by giving him a portion of food five times greater than the others. The purpose of this test was to see if they were going to show contempt for their youngest brother just as they burned with anger towards Joseph after their father's display of favoritism towards him. According to Genesis 35:16 – 20, Benjamin was already born by the time Joseph was sold into slavery at the age of 17, but Benjamin was just a toddler by that point. Now, Joseph is testing if they treated Benjamin the same way they treated him.

There's something important to notice in Genesis 43. Reuben

was willing to put his two sons to death for the sake of Benjamin's safety and Judah was willing to guard Benjamin with his life. These are conversations Joseph did not hear, but they were indicative of men who had deeply repented of their sinful ways from 20 years prior. Repentance is the soil by which the seed of forgiveness can be planted and bear the fruit of restored relationships.

THE THIRD TEST

In Genesis 44, we see Joseph administer his final test to his brothers by planting his diviner's cup into Benjamin's sack in order to hold him captive as a slave to Egypt. This passage has caused some to question whether or not Joseph actually practiced divination and the short answer is no. First of all, there is nothing in Joseph's lifestyle as recorded in Scripture that would support this view, and secondly, the presence of a diviner's cup was common among Pharaoh's officials.

The important aspect to this passage is Judah's response. Judah, 20 years earlier, was the very one who proposed selling his younger brother Joseph as a slave (Genesis 37:26-27). Now, he is willing to substitute his life for his younger brother Benjamin. Joseph has now seen his older brother Judah go from rebellious to repentant; selfish to selfless. Joseph has all the evidence he needs to know if restoration and reconciliation are possible. This leads us to his response in Genesis 45.

RESTORATION

Genesis 45 is a beautiful passage. It is the climax of 20 years worth of hardship, separation, guilt, and unconfessed sin which, after necessary repentance, led to restoration and joy. Repentance is the soil by which the seed of forgiveness can be planted and bear the fruit of restored relationships. Forgiveness is a one-sided event. As God's people, we are commanded to forgive no matter how horrific the offense toward us was. The reason for that is because a person's offense toward us is minuscule compared to our offense toward God. Reconciliation; however, is a two-way street. Forgiveness does not equal a restored relationship. Just as Joseph tested the hearts of his brothers before he allowed restoration so we need to prayerfully and wisely test the hearts of those whom we have a broken relationship with before we can begin rebuilding that relationship.

LET'S PRAY, *"Dear God, I thank You for never giving up on restoring Your relationship with me. I don't deserve Your love, forgiveness, and blessings, but I am extremely grateful to experience them. Help me to exemplify You in seeking the restoration of broken relationships in my life so You can get the glory. Please give me the wisdom to know what to do and the courage to do it. I ask this in the name of Jesus. Amen."*

ACTION POINT

I know the phrase "broken relationship" can be emotionally charged and sensitive. Perhaps someone was quickly brought to mind like your spouse, a family member, a friend, or coworker. Your Action Point for today is simple, difficult, but rewarding: Initiate restoring a broken relationship. Here's a plan to help you get started.

1. **Pray** - Ask God to show you one person He wants you to starting restoring your relationship with. Then, write their name down somewhere that you'll see consistently so you can begin praying for them consistently.
2. **Speak** - Humble yourself first even if they are the sole

offender. Confess your part of the conflict and apologize for any harm you caused them. Control your emotions before, during, and after the conversation. Remember, we want to make the situation better, not worse.

3. **Wait** - Just as technique, toil, and time are used in the growth of a healthy garden so it is with growing a healthy relationship even if the weeds, storms, and abuse of life have destroyed it. Be patient, do your part, and let God handle the rest.

I would love to hear how this goes for you and walk alongside you in this matter, so please feel free to contact me! I'm praying for you and the person the Lord has brought to your mind that you will begin this process with. I'm confident that though this will be uncomfortable, you and God will be blessed by it in the end.

DAY TWENTY-SEVEN

GENESIS 45:16 - 46:27

"Everyone will be forgotten, nothing we do will make any difference, and all good endeavors, even the best, will come to naught. Unless there is God. If the God of the Bible exists, and there is a True Reality beneath and behind this one, and this life is not the only life, then every good endeavor, even the simplest ones, pursued in response to God's calling, can matter forever." - Timothy Keller, Pastor & Author

FAITHFULNESS LEADS TO FAVOR

Joseph's faithfulness to God led to his favor with the Pharaoh. It's noteworthy that Joseph's godly character and skillful administration had such an influence on Pharaoh that he would be so quick to bless Joseph's family with the best of the land of Egypt. Solomon says in Proverbs 22:29, "Do you see a man who excels in his work? He will stand before kings; He will not stand before unknown men." The combination of Joseph's skill and God's sovereignty led him to that position and to be in such favor with

Pharaoh. The more you depend on Christ and the more skillful you become in your work the more you too will stand before men and women of prominence. If the Lord wills, you will network with them, have favor with them, and take those God-given opportunities to not only add value to those around you, but ultimately advance the Kingdom of God.

FAITHFULNESS LEADS TO FRUITFULNESS

The faithfulness of Joseph, and those who came before him, led to fruitfulness. Like many great works of God, Israel had a slow beginning. From the time God called Abraham, it took at least 25 years to add one son; Isaac. It took Isaac 60 years to add another son; Jacob. It took Jacob about 50 years to add 12 sons and 1 daughter. In 430 years this family of 70 will grow to about 2 million people. You might be walking in your calling, but wondering why the results aren't exactly what you expected. Be patient my friend, stay faithful, stay perseverant, and God just might go above and beyond your expectations of what you could ever ask for or think of.

CALLING AND GIFTING

So far in our journey through Genesis we have seen God call upon specific individuals for a specific task and you get the opportunity to share in that spiritual lineage. Here's a quick story of how I realized God's calling upon my life. When I was 19 years old, completing my education at Calvary Chapel Bible College (CCBC), I was starting an Affiliate CCBC in the Imperial Valley. One Sunday morning during Service Pete Mallinger, our Senior Pastor, was giving announcements and sometime during that I heard, "… and you guys can see Pastor Sean regarding that…" This caught me by surprise because it was the first time I had ever heard the words "Pastor" and "Sean" put together. My mentor,

Pastor Pete, was watching God use me to care for souls, lead ministries, counsel, disciple, etc. Now, there have been a time or two where I had desires to stray from my calling, but God swiftly and clearly brought me back. Feel free to contact me directly for those stories!

You see, mankind doesn't ordain anyone, nor can they place a calling upon someone, they simply acknowledge God's calling upon a person's life. God has a specific plan for you to fulfill, gifting for you to use, and a calling to answer. Do you know your role in the Body of Christ? Do you know the specific legacy God wants you to leave behind when you enter His kingdom? I recommend the following passages to discover your calling and gifting: Romans 12:3 - 8, 1st Corinthians 12 - 14, and Ephesians 4:11 - 15.

LET'S PRAY, *"Dear God, thank You that before I was born, You already had a plan for my life. Please help me to walk faithfully in that plan. Please show me what You want me to do. Reveal my calling and gifting for Your name's sake and to advance Your kingdom. I ask this in the name of Jesus. Amen."*

∼

ACTION POINT

All throughout Genesis we have seen God's Plan of Redemption unfolding as a result of His sovereignty and man's responsibility to walk in their God-given calling.

You may be confident with your position in the Body of Christ or you may still be trying to discover what your calling is. Your Action Point for today is to begin that discovery or to refine it by doing at least one of the following:

- Have a meeting with your Pastor to have them pray

with you, counsel you, and discover your calling with you. I am also personally at your service, so feel free to contact me directly and I would love to help!

- Take a Spiritual Gifts Test. I recommend using the one at Lifeway.com. This is not a guaranteed way of discovering your calling and gifting, but it has been helpful to many of God's people.
- Set aside time consistently to pray and fast asking God to reveal His specific will and calling on your life.

DAY TWENTY-EIGHT

GENESIS 46:28 - 47:31

"So you see, organizing in fact is not about the trappings of neatness like those cute file folders or plastic bins. It's not some rigid system being imposed upon us that we fear will stifle our creativity. In the end, organizing is about making room for the things in our life that are truly important: our life priorities. Take it from me, I'm a mother of two small children and a business owner in an ever-changing economy...practicing order is a commitment. I honor and practice order because it helps me to live the life I want. In my line of work, I've learned that if you can embrace this truth you can get a break-through: organizing is a not a chore, it's a choice. It's a moment-by-moment practice of better life management that will bring you freedom!" - Vicki Norris, Professional Organizer and Entrepreneur

JOSEPH'S ORGANIZATION

Out of the goodness of God Jacob is reunited with his son Joseph after 22 years and will live 17 years in Egypt to. Jacob will also have the blessing of seeing his grandchildren Manasseh and Ephraim. Joseph's dreams came true and God's prophetic vision fulfilled. As the family of Israel is being settled in Goshen the famine in the land becomes more severe. Joseph's administration, organization, and leadership are needed more than ever for the survival of many.

Joseph's organizational skills were refined over many years from serving as a shepherd, a house manager for Potiphar, a supervisor of prisoners, and now 2nd to Pharaoh. As his position increased, so did his responsibility. The same is true for you and me; if we aim for higher positions in work, ministry, military, etc. then we need to be prepared for the higher responsibility that comes with it.

Through Joseph's wisdom, by the end of the famine, Pharaoh possessed all of the money in Egypt, owned all of the people, and all of their property (Except that of the priests). Farmers had to pay an annual tax of a fifth of their harvest as well. Not only had Joseph saved multitudes from starvation, but he shifted the whole economic system to where Pharaoh was in control of everything. God sovereignly positioned Joseph to create a stable environment for the family of Jacob to grow into the nation of Israel that we see in Exodus.

Organization and discipline are Biblical Values (Proverbs 13:4; 1st Corinthians 14:40) while laziness and slothful management are sin (Proverbs 24:30 - 34; Matthew 25:14 - 30). Our lives and the lives of those around us would benefit from us improving our management, organization, discipline, and leadership skills to the glory of God! So let's make an effort to do that today.

LET'S PRAY, *"Dear God, thank You for being the ultimate example of order. By Your infinite wisdom, power, and organization you breathed the Universe into existence and designed it with unmatched complexity and harmony. Please help me to be more disciplined and organized; not just for the sake of productivity, but primarily for You to gain more glory from my life. I ask this in the name of Jesus. Amen."*

ACTION POINT

Organization is not only practical, it's Biblical. So, your Action Point for today is to begin implementing or improving your organizational efficiency. Here are 5 ways to get started:

- **Start a To-Do List**. I have personally been using a To-Do list app of some kind on my phone for years and it keeps my life organized; both personally and professionally. Currently I'm using the App "Microsoft To-Do" (Formerly Wunderlist). Experiment with different options and stick with what's best for you.
- **Give Everything a Home**. Time is wasted when looking for things. So, take look around your home, your work, your car, and make sure all of your items have a home. The real key is not just getting organized, but staying organized.
- **Declutter Regularly and Resist Hoarding**. This is touchy for some because items can have sentimental value. Schedule time to take inventory of your things to see what you can sell or give away.
- **Delegate**. Stop doing more of what others can do and start doing less of what only you can do in your family, work, and ministry. Disciple, train, and empower others to learn new skills and take some of your tasks so you can focus on higher priorities and higher leverage opportunities.
- **Create Systems**. This is a big one and will take time to master. Creating a system (AKA "Playbook") for what

you do in your personal life, family, work, or ministry will lower your decision fatigue, create more time to do what you love, and increase your overall efficiency to accomplish the goals you want to. I encourage you to check out Chandler Bolt's teaching on this by going to YouTube and searching "Chandler Bolt - Creating Systems".

DAY TWENTY-NINE

GENESIS 48:1 - 49:33

"Believe me when I say I know how tough it is being a man and a father today. You feel like you give and work and struggle and there's never enough of you to go around. The pressures are unrelenting. And yet you are so important that you are nearly irreplaceable in the lives of your children—especially your son. Fatherhood is a privilege given by God, and with that privilege comes the power to impact lives. Exercised responsibly for good, that power can lead to God's blessing on you and your family." - Rick Johnson, Founder of Better Dads

JACOB SPEAKING OVER HIS SONS

We now see the final words of Jacob as he speaks both blessing and prophesy over his 12 sons. There were many times where Jacob failed as a father, but now in his old age, he is fulfilling his role as a father and spiritual leader. Here is some insight into what Jacob speaks over his sons:

- **Reuben** - The sin Reuben committed 20 years earlier cost him his birthright which resulted in Joseph's sons, Ephraim and Manasseh, to receive the birthright and become heads of their own tribes (1st Chronicles 5:1).
- **Simeon** - This tribe's portion of land was within the midst of Judah's territory (Joshua 19:1); however, Simeon did not grow as rapidly as Judah and seems to have dispersed across multiple territories (1 Chronicles 4:38–43; 2 Chronicles 15:8–9). This is consistent with Jacob's prophecy concerning Simeon and his brother Levi: "I will disperse them in Jacob, and scatter them in Israel."
- **Levi** - The tribe of the priesthood. The tribe of Levi stood by Moses during the golden calf incident at Mount Sinai (Exodus 32:25–29), later took their place as ministers in the tabernacle, and later the Temple; Levitical duties were extensive (Read Leviticus!) Levi had no tribal territory—the Lord was the tribe's inheritance (Numbers 18:19–20); however, they did receive pasture lands for their cattle (Joshua 21). Some notable tribesmen are Moses, Aaron, John the Baptist, and Barnabas.
- **Judah** - The prophecy over Judah, whose name means "praise", is a shining example of God's grace. Though Judah had stains of sin on his life, God used his tribe to bring kings, godly leaders, and ultimately the Messiah, Jesus the Christ.
- **Zebulun** - The tribe of Zebulun settled in the land between the Sea of Galilee and the Mediterranean Sea which had an important route for trade because it was an intersection for the coastal Sea (West), Jerusalem (South), Sea of Galilee (East), and Damascus (North). They were also faithful to King David by supplying the

largest number of soldiers from a single tribe (1st Chronicles 12:33).

- **Issachar** - This tribe was 3rd in size according to the Numbers 26 census. They worked hard, but produced no big name heroes. Remember, not everyone is called to be a Judah, David, Billy Graham, Chuck Smith, etc. However, your calling is just as important because faithfulness to God is more important than the fame of man.

- **Dan** - This tribe supplied one of the most prominent judges; Samson (Judges 13:2). Dan was a troublesome tribe that did in fact make the "rider (Israel) fall backward". They introduced idolatry into Israel (Judges.18:30), Jeroboam set up his idolatrous golden calves in Dan (1st Kings 12:26-30), and later Dan became a center for idol worship in Israel (Amos 8:14). Dan is left out of the listing of tribes regarding 144,000 in Revelation 7:5-8, but is the 1st tribe listed in Ezekiel 48 for the Millennial Kingdom

- **Gad** - This tribe settled on the East side of the Jordan with Reuben and the "half tribe of Manasseh" making them an easy target for enemy troops to attack them. The ultimate fulfillment of Jacob's prophesy will come during the Millennial Kingdom according to Ezekiel 48:28.

- **Asher** - Moses said in Deuteronomy 33:24, "Asher is the most blessed of sons; let him be favored by his brothers, and let him dip his foot in oil." The tribe of Asher settled down as an agricultural people along the Mediterranean Sea just North of Zebulun. To this day that area is known for its olive groves.

- **Naphtali** - This tribe settled in a key area near the Sea of Galilee. The prophecy over Naphtali is fitting and clearly fulfilled by having the Messiah do much of His teaching in their region of Galilee; certainly beautiful words were used that came from God Himself in the flesh (Matthew 4:12 - 16)

- **Joseph** - When speaking over his son, Jacob used the word "bless" or "blessing" 6x. The word "fruitful" refers to 2 things: 1) His political, social, and financial success while 2nd in command over Egypt, and 2) his son Ephraim. Ephraim means "I shall be doubly fruitful" and this tribe would grow to have a large territory (Joshua 17:14-18).
- **Benjamin** - Why compare Benjamin with a "ravenous wolf"? Here are at least 3 reasons: 1) When you read about Benjamin going against all of Israel during a civil war in Judges 19 – 21, you certainly see a ravenous wolf in action. 2) King Saul was a Benjamite who tried to kill David several times and ruthlessly murdered everybody in the priestly city of Nob (1st Samuel 22:6). 3) Other Benjamites known for their ferocity were Abner (2nd Sam. 2:23), Sheba (2nd Sam. 20), Shimei (2nd Sam. 16:5-14), and Saul of Tarsus, who was a Benjamite, ravenously attacked the early Church (Phil. 3:5)

FIGHTING FOR FAITHFUL FATHERHOOD

History, statistics, and mankind's personal experience prove that Fathers play a key role in the overall development of the child. Satan has attacked the family unit, specifically fatherhood, because he knows the monopoly effect of damage that can bring. Today's Action Point is specifically designed for Fathers and Father-Figures, but the Biblical values are applicable to everyone. Like Jacob, we are not perfect, but are still called to be the spiritual leader and speak into the lives of our kids with words and actions.

· · ·

LET'S PRAY, *"Dear God, thank You for being my Heavenly Father. Thank You for unconditionally loving me and persistently training me to be the child of God I'm called to be. Please help me to faithfully lead my biological kids and spiritual kids with Your Biblical values. I ask this in the name of Jesus. Amen."*

∼

ACTION POINT

Whether you have biological kids or spiritual kids (Those in the faith younger than you), the following Action Point is to help you lead them in 6 Biblically important areas:

- **Physically** (3rd John 1:2) - Eat healthy, drink plenty of water, get enough sleep, exercise consistently, and honor God by managing well the one body He gave you so that you can serve with greater quantity of time and quality of life.
- **Educationally** (Proverbs 18:15) - Always be teachable, constantly aim to grow in your personal development, family overall health, work, ministry, etc.
- **Occupationally** (Colossians 3:23) - Christians should aim to outperform, outsmart, and outwork everyone; not for their own glory, but so that people would see your good works and glorify your Father in Heaven (Matthew 5:16)
- **Financially** (Proverbs 13:22) - Get out of debt, build an emergency fund, invest for the future, and give generously to the glory of God. I strongly suggest following Dave Ramsey's advice and getting on 7 Baby Steps. Go to DaveRamsey.com to get started.
- **Relationally** (Mark 12:31) - Demonstrate respect, humility, and selflessness to your kids in the way you

interact with others. Remember, your relationship with God determines your relationship with everyone else, which brings us to the final value.

- **Spiritually** (Deuteronomy 6:4 - 9) - Consistently demonstrate and teach what it means to pursue loving God with all of your heart, soul, mind, and strength. Open your mouth and let God use your voice to speak life and love into your kids.

DAY THIRTY

GENESIS 50:1 - 26

"There are many stories in the Bible about achieving goals. The people of the Bible were not complacent when it came to setting and achieving their goals. Some of my favorite examples are Noah building the ark, Moses leading the Israelite's to the promised land, Paul planting churches and helping to bring many people to faith while growing the church exponentially. There's one thing we need to realize about goal setting as servants of God. Like Noah, Moses, and Paul, our goals need to be according to the will of God, and always in submission to His leadership." - Cecily Joy, Founder of thegracetogrow.com

PARALLELS BETWEEN JOSEPH & JESUS

It would be negligent of me to not mention God's divine authorship by showing the parallels between Joseph and Jesus. In reality, the Book of Genesis ends with hope; hope that one day a "greater than Joseph" would be raised from the grave. Joseph was real man in history, but God also used his life as a shadow of the substance to come; a foreshadowing of Someone greater who would make His debut; Jesus Christ the Savior of the world. Here are some, not all, parallels between Joseph and Jesus that God orchestrated in advance. I highly recommend you check out the verse references for more details:

1. Loved by his father (Genesis 37:3; Matthew 3:17)
2. Envied and hated unjustly (Genesis 37:4; Mark 15:10)
3. A "root out off dry ground" (Genesis 37:3; Isaiah 53:2)
4. He foretold that one day he would rule (Genesis 37:7; Matthew 26:64)
5. Accused of being a dreamer, deluded, and crazy (Genesis 37:19; Mark 3:21)
6. Sent by the father for the brothers' well-being (Genesis 37:14; Luke 20:13)
7. Willingly sought out his brothers (Genesis 37:17; John 1:11)
8. Rejected and condemned to die (Genesis 37:18; Luke 23:31)
9. Stripped of his clothing (Genesis 37:23; Matthew 27:28)
10. Thrown into a pit (Genesis 37:24; Matthew 12:40)
11. Sold for silver into the hands of Gentiles (Genesis 37:28; Matthew 26:15)
12. Raised from the pit (Genesis 37:28; 1st Corinthians 15:4)
13. Became a servant (Genesis 39:1 - 2; Philippians 2:7)
14. Everything he did prospered (Genesis 39:3; Isaiah 53:10)
15. Resisted temptation (Genesis 39:7 - 12; Hebrews 4:15)
16. Falsely accused (Genesis 39:17 - 18; Matthew 26:60)
17. Unjustly held with other sinners (Genesis 39:20; Luke 23:33)
18. Promised freedom to a condemned man (Genesis 40:13; Luke 23:43)

19. Accurately foretold the future (Genesis 41:13; John 13:19)
20. Great counselor (Genesis 41:39; Isaiah 9:6)
21. Promoted to honor and given a new name (Genesis 41:41 - 45; Philippians 2:9)
22. All people are commanded to bow to him (Genesis 41:43; Philippians 2:10)
23. Provided for all in need (Genesis 41:57; John 6:35)
24. His people did not recognize him (Genesis 42:8; John 14:9)
25. Revelation and reconciliation (Genesis 45:3 - 9; Romans 11:26)

GOALS AND GOD

As we begin to close the Book of Genesis together we have seen God work through the lives of many men and women. Some made plans to honor the LORD and some did not. As we reflect on the life, death, successes, failures, good, and bad of the lives recorded in Genesis, it makes me think about setting and achieving God-honoring goals. There is a supernatural balance between man's responsibility and God's sovereignty throughout the Bible. God will do His part, but we must also be faithful to do ours. The goals achieved by God's people in Scripture and Church History were not by accident, unplanned, or reached through inconsistent behaviors. You and I have the opportunity accomplish amazing and world-changing goals for the glory of God, but that takes prayer, fasting, the counsel of God's word, focused intentionality, strategic planning, and consistent behavior.

LET'S PRAY, *"Dear God, thank You for the Book of Genesis. Thank You for the examples of men and women You've used throughout history. Help me to hear Your voice on what You want me to accomplish in life.*

Please give me the wisdom to know what to do, the courage to start, and the discipline to finish. I ask this in the name of Jesus. Amen."

ACTION POINT

Yesterday we talked about leading by example in 6 areas: Physical, Educational, Occupational, Financial, Relational, and Spiritual. Today, your Action Point is to build upon those by setting a goal in each of those areas. Here's how you can get started:

- **Plan** - First, write down at least one goal in each of the 6 areas mentioned above. Be as detailed as possible and be specific about when you want to accomplish that goal.
- **Share** - There's power in numbers. Share your goals with those closest to you. This will help you by having a support system around you to pray for you, encourage you, and keep you accountable to take those goals to the finish line.
- **Accomplish** - Get moving! Start making moves, even if they're small, towards accomplishing your goals. Give yourself grace when you fall and just get back up. Don't give up, keep the goal in mind, and remember, you're doing this to honor God more than yourself.

I would love to help you accomplish your goals so feel free to contact me and let me know how I can pray for you and support you!

CONGRATULATIONS!

Congratulations on completing the 30-Day In His Presence Challenge through the Book of Genesis! I hope it has been an enriching experience for you and it would mean a lot to me if you to go to Amazon.com to rate and review letting other people know your feedback.

I encourage you to now take a step of faith. Prayerfully consider leading one person or a Small Group through this 30-Day In His Presence Challenge. If you would like tips on leading a Small Group, please go to the Introduction page.

ALSO BY SEAN ARVISO

FIND THESE BOOKS ON AMAZON IN
PAPERBACK, E-BOOK, AND AUDIOBOOK

Made in the USA
San Bernardino, CA
15 July 2020